SOUL
SHINE

SOUL SHINE

Excavate Your Light and Claim Your Soul's Purpose

created by
Women Who Choose to Shine

Original cover art: Kelsey Wyatt

ISBN 978-1-913590-71-0 Paperback
ISBN 978-1-913590-72-7 Ebook

The Unbound Press
www.theunboundpress.com

Hey unbound one!

Welcome to this magical book brought to you by The Unbound Press.

At The Unbound Press we believe that when women write freely from the fullest expression of who they are, it can't help but activate a feeling of deep connection and transformation in others. When we come together, we become more and we're changing the world, one book at a time!

This book has been carefully crafted by both the contributors and publisher with the intention of inspiring you to move ever more deeply into who you truly are.

We hope that this book helps you to connect with your Unbound Self and that you feel called to pass it on to others who want to live a more fully expressed life.

With much love,
Nicola Humber

Founder of The Unbound Press
www.theunboundpress.com

Dedication to All Who Want Their Soul to Shine

This book is dedicated to all the women
who have dimmed their light while allowing others to shine.
All the women who became people-pleasers and door mats.
All the women who question if they should excavate their light
and claim what has always been their Soul's Purpose.
All the women who are ready to slough off the "shoulds" and
embody the "want tos."
This Book is Dedicated to
ALL WOMEN!

CONTENTS

Foreword for
Inspiring Your Soul Shine

As I began to excavate the layers of societal demands, a long list of "shoulds," all the trauma that I have held onto, and all the responsibilities I shouldered that were not mine to bear, I began to see a light that I never even knew I had. With the reality that I have dimmed my authentic self since I was eight years old, I began to wonder about the breadth of shade from women, and I realized we all have diminished ourselves at some point during our lives. In that moment, clinging to the kitchen sink and the certainty that every woman has, in some way, dimmed themselves for others, I decided that this extinguishment was no longer an option. How many of us have missed the opportunity to shine at all?

It was here that I decided it was my duty, my soul's purpose, to shine a spotlight on this issue in our world.

As you read the following memoirs, take the time to question yourself, and recognize where you are hiding your light, your gifts, and your purpose. Also, where you may have contributed to dimming others.

This world is full of blaming others for the demise of oneself. We blame the patriarchy. We blame all the ~isms that divide people. We blame societal roles and rules. This is putting us all in tiny boxes until we find ourselves, darkened, all alone in this minuscule, fenced-in area because we identify every aspect of ourselves to make us feel unique and special. The truth is, like fingerprints, we are all unique, with a special shine all our own, a soul's purpose specific to our very DNA. Once we realize this, we can stop drawing those lines and building those fences and start igniting each other with love, unity, and reciprocity.

So, it is my hope that you find a piece of yourself in each chapter and allow each discovery to ignite your own excavation to your lost light.

Start Shining!

Women ...

As women, are we all sisters, together

Or are we White sisters, Black sisters, Hispanic sisters, etc.?

Divided by our culture?

Are we women working together to lift each other up, support each other, love, believe in, listen to each other?

Or are we divided by our beliefs, heritage, finances, even hair color?

Are we sisters striving to be our best selves, reaching down and pulling the next woman up?

Or are we competing, trampling on one another to be above, more in the spotlight, and collecting more followers?

Are we friends and sisters through the good, the bad, the ugly-cries, and beautiful celebrations?

Or do we crush each other for the next hot, rich man that comes along?

Do we help each other believe in ourselves, our power, and incredible, unique abilities?

Or do we believe only one can be the best, and it can only be YOU?

Are you a sister in solidarity to shine and allow others to join you in shining, burning brighter with every hand joined, knowing we are truly in power and not allowing anyone to create doubt in who we are and who we are meant to be?

Be the one who reaches down to pull a sister up with you and not the one stepping on her head to get above her.

For I Am The Light

Standing at my kitchen sink, just a month before my 50th birthday, it hit me like a lightning bolt. I have been dimming my light since I was eight years old. When this memory slammed into my heart, I almost crumbled to the floor. How could I — a strong middle child, Scorpio, cheerleader — have lived, barely burning for the past 42 years? But the reality is, I have, and I did.

Soul work is one of the most difficult journeys I have ever taken. These moments when epiphanies take you out at the knees, when you want to pull on the reins and scream, "STOP! NO, I could not have done that! I thought I was strong and knew who I am!" Have I? Have I ever known who I was? Who I am?

At eight years old, I was sitting on the concrete stairs at our local pool beside my cousin, waiting to be divided by skill level for swim lessons. Having had several swim classes before, I was fairly skilled in the water. My cousin, however, had not had lessons and feared being in the beginner class alone. I sat back with her.

I got a little dimmer that day. And, at the kitchen sink that September morning, my whole life of flickering flashed before me. My mind swirled through Junior High and High School, friends and boyfriends and all the places I hid so I would not outshine another, especially another girl/woman in my life. Why are we, as women, socialized to be pitted against one another, instead of lifting each other up, supporting and loving each other? In turn, why do we feel we cannot shine our unique light out to the world, fully and uneclipsed? Like a fingerprint, we are all unique in our shine. These are the questions I ask today and the realizations I am sending out into the world so every woman can shine from her soul, from birth to death!

As I grasped the kitchen sink that cool fall morning, I distinctly acknowledged my most significant extinguishment of my fiery light. At the beginning of ninth grade, my best friend turned on me because a few guys that she liked, liked me. She even gave my phone number to one of these guys. It was a confusing age, 14, beginning to shed my adolescent body that was always a bit chubby and starting to come into a more womanly, fit body. I started getting attention from the guys in our school and, of course, I liked it. I was a cheerleader and always outgoing, always making new friends. But I thought she and I had a bond that would last through everything. But, boys came between us.

Because of her reaction to the boys liking me, I began to shrink, dull my shine, and fade into the background of school life. I thought I could reclaim our friendship, if she could see that I became small and no longer outshined her. I thought this is what women do because we are not supposed to be brighter than our friends; we are not supposed to stand out and be unique and bold.

From this moment, in 1984, until that September morning in 2020, I held onto this mentality with such determination and fortitude that I almost missed my chance to shine at all!

In 1987, I chose to date a guy that had dropped out of high school, and only a few of my peers even knew. I thought I was safe to date him because no other girl in high school would be jealous of me for dating a guy outside of the selection at high school. During the four years we dated, I got smaller, duller, and almost non-existent. He controlled everything we did and everyone we hung out with. *I let him.* I was trying to do all the "shoulds" that I thought were right. I worked. I studied. I knelt to him and his every whim. We spent my money. He did what he wanted to. He controlled me. He used me. He cheated on me. He got his ex-girlfriend pregnant and lied to me about that. Manipulated her to lie to me also. AND I got engaged to him. *WHAT???* Yes, I was so small that I did not value myself enough to see what he was doing. This guy, who I thought was my soulmate, was only a lesson in all that love should not be. During these four years, he molded me, manipulated me, chastened me. He constrained me from loving myself, owning my light, and growing as my authentic self. *I let him.* This is the hardest thing to realize. *I let him.*

Once we broke up, I was lost in my dark pit of despair. It was dark inside my head, inside my body, and in my outlook. I ended up *getting over* him but never truly processing the trauma that he left in his wake.

As my memories moved past him to college, I allowed a friend to shine and leave me in her shadow. *I let her.* It seems that I was drawn to friendships where I "knew my place." Shadows were my safe place. I did not have to put myself out there, as I just hung out with the shiny, loud people. Little did I know that the shiny people I had chosen as friends were a bit narcissistic and a whole lot toxic. I have many regrets within this college friendship as I basically rolled out the red carpet for her to stand in her wants and needs while I quietly witnessed her dancing in the spotlight that I was holding.

Sigh. Why would I do this? Oh yes, all the conditioning I had absorbed and self-taught since I was eight years old ... *That is why.*

Then I became a wife and mother. All the societal "shoulds" landed in my lap with a heavy thud. My grateful heart was filled with a beautiful home, the ability and blessing to stay home to raise my kids and be a wife. With such enormous blessings comes great responsibility to everyone ... everyone but me, that is. I put them first, always! I would not change this for one minute. My kids have greatly benefited from my constant presence and guidance. I am, for the most part, proud of who I am as a mom!

So, let me tell you about being a wife. My husband works incredibly hard to provide for our family and always has. So much gratitude!

However, because of this, I felt a huge sense of obligation to bend over backwards for his every need. And since I never truly worked *through* all I went through with my previous boyfriend, I rarely even asked myself what I wanted or needed. When he began to express greater desires than I was sure of giving, I once again began to shrink, dim, and flicker in all that I thought I was. I thought, if I gave more, became thinner, and did all the things, he would be happy with me. I got quieter, busied myself with anything and everything, and grew smaller and dimmer as he grew bolder in his desires.

After moving into a new house and settling in, it became clear that he was no longer emotionally, physically, or mentally present with me. I witnessed myself drinking, shrinking, and becoming more depressed. It was like I was witnessing a slow-motion train wreck, from outside myself. In June 2014, I found proof of what I already knew. He was having an affair. I felt non-existent once again and fell into that deep, dark pit of despair. I no longer could even see any light, much less shine from my own soul, my own heart.

As we worked through his infidelity, I held on tight to being a victim, clung tightly to my hurt and covered it with a black cloud that followed me like a lost pup. I owned my depression, my hatred for him, his mistress, and myself, my resentment, and my right to be hurt by all that transpired. For six years, I denied myself any light. I reveled in my darkness. I hid so much from so many. I resented anyone who appeared to be happy. Dim, dark, and extinguished was my safe place. Why did it even matter anyway? All of my "shoulds" were just notches on my dying tree of life.

After my daughter read my journal and my son confronted me, I woke up and decided I no longer wanted to live in the muck of resentment and pain. I began counseling, reading, and journaling on healing, instead of wallowing in pain, and I began to furiously dig into the depth of my past. Books and journals filled my nightstand, my office, and my car. The yoga classes I taught began to fill with the meaning and inspiration rising up from deep within myself. Counselling left me refreshed, rather than drained and swollen-eyed. I heard laughter instead of crying. Meditation began to have meaning and resolve instead of a battle to just be still for five minutes. My steps got lighter, and my world started to get a little brighter.

This did not happen overnight, not even over a year. Going on three years now, I've begun to crave the light, the sun, and even the brightness of the full moon! I now know that nothing is against me and that all the struggles and hurt that others "put on me" were never mine at all. I stopped asking, "How could you do it to me?" and started asking,

"What is this challenging me to learn?" and "Does this relationship still deserve the space it takes up in my life?"

In 2020, I set an intention to *"LET GO!"* and boy, did the Universe respond. I let go of so much that I had nothing left to cover or dull my shine. At 50, I finally sloughed off all the layers of expectations, societal conformity, decades of pain and self-doubt, and traumas of all sorts and sizes. I began to release all those self-created limitations and see the vastness of my abilities, potential, and love.

I am no longer that eight-year-old girl sitting on those concrete steps holding space for others' needs.

I am no longer the fourteen-year-old holding herself back from all she wanted.

I am no longer the girlfriend who is the doormat for you to wipe your feet on and welcome you back time and again, regardless of the muck you brought to me.

I am no longer the friend who holds the spotlight as you enter every room.

And I am no longer the wife that bends and molds myself to meet you where you are without questioning what I need.

What I am is my pure, work-in-progress, scarred and bruised, authentic self, who shines from my heart and soul. If I feel myself beginning to dim or dull, I take a step back, get a clear view and decide where to go from the new perspective. Finally, I am whom I was always meant to be. I am living my soul's purpose and growing every day into all that I know I am destined to be. The truth is, I could have been a shining bright light all my life, but then, I would not be the person I was born to be. If this path had been easy, with few obstacles, I would be shallow, limited, and boring. How dull would that be?

Even though I held onto the kitchen sink that September morning, I let go of more than you could imagine, and now, I shine bright, intentionally, and authentically from my heart, from my soul. And I am forever grateful for the journey that brought me to this stage where I do not need the spotlight, for I *am* the light!

About Carrie Myers, MSW, RYT

Carrie J Myers, MSW, is a yoga instructor and former studio owner, poet and program developer. A native of Asheville, North Carolina, and a mother of three, Carrie has been writing since she was ten years old. Most of her work is poetry which reflects the phases of her life and helps her process her journey along the way. As a yoga instructor, she discovers new ways to dig deep into her subconscious, pulling from her practice the words that held higher meaning and growth. As she puts her work out into the world, she hopes to inspire change in the hearts and souls of her readers while holding space for each interpretation to resonate with each soul's purpose. Carrie is passionate about creating and recognizing the beauty in the mess that life can throw at us. Her goal is to help readers rediscover their authentic selves and revive, create, and discover their light within. Her passion is people — inspiring them, loving them, and helping them heal. She has just begun her writing career with a poem published in *#2020 Vision, "Unbound Perspective from a Year Like No Other,"* and a full collection of poetry in *Soul Confetti, Celebrating Life's Lessons.*

@cjmyerspoet
carriemyersauthor.com
yourselfprogram.com

What I Want
My Younger Self to Know

Dear Younger Michelle,

You have always loved to write. As a child and teenager, you wrote countless short stories and poems. As the years went by, you wrote in a journal for yourself, but writing short stories and poems fell away. However, always in your mind is the thought, "Someday, I'm going to write a book. Even though I have no idea what it's going to be about, someday, I will write a book."

Fast forward to October 2018, you attended a workshop that would change the course of your life. On that particular Saturday, you had the opportunity to choose between three different events, and for whatever reason, the Empowerment Workshop called to you. At the time of this workshop, you were at the start of a great questioning period. *What am I doing with my life? What am I going to have to show for my life? When I'm old, am I going to look back on my life and wonder what could have been?*

You attended the workshop, and it wasn't until you were thanking one of the facilitators at the end that you broke down in tears. Seemingly out of nowhere, the tears were just flowing, and you really were not sure what exactly it was all about. Something within you was cracked open, and as you drove home later that day, you experienced one of your first "downloads" — Project Worthiness.

The idea came to you that each month you will choose a "focus word." *What does the word really mean to me? What books can I read about it? What workshops or webinars can I attend around my theme word?* Thoughts and ideas about where this project could go started coming to you seemingly out of nowhere — even when you were not consciously thinking about it. You saw the possibility of promoting products related to the theme word — perhaps even a workbook or book about it.

In January 2019, you officially started your project: "Project Worthiness: A Year to Discover and Empower Myself." You shared on social media about your focus word of the month and how you were exploring it. Little did you know about the wild and crazy ride this Project would take you on over the next few years. Your beliefs about yourself and the world would be cracked open in so many ways. Throw in a global pandemic, and it got even crazier. More came up about who you really are, what your true values are, and how you want to show up in the world. Like you'd named this project, thoughts about your worthiness would come up. *Who am I to be doing this? Is what I'm doing with this Project Worthiness going to be of any actual value? Do I have what it takes to make these dreams come true? Am I worthy of making these dreams come true?*

So, you started out on your journey, and some of the first words were *Authenticity, Gratitude,* and *Purposeful.*

In December 2019, during a session with your coach, the discussion moved to the word *Rebel.* At first, you did not identify with this word at all. To you, a rebel was someone who didn't follow the rules or the law, someone who usually ended up getting arrested. But as you gave it more thought, you realized that it could have a different meaning. It could be about questioning the beliefs and thought patterns you have about yourself and the world. It could be about realizing what no longer holds truth and validity for yourself, things you need to let go of to move forward in your life. It is the first step on the path to elevating yourself.

It's now May 2020, and after much debate, you chose the word *Elevate.* Right after posting about it on Instagram, you saw an ad for an upcoming online summit happening later that month. After a couple of days in that summit, you realize just how right you were in choosing the word *Elevate.* Your whole energy shifted for those few weeks of the summit. You felt lighter and felt a new sense of direction that you had not felt in a long time. Even two years later, you would still feel the effects of that summit as you made connections with an amazing group of women in the online space.

So, my dear younger self, a few thoughts for you:

1. Trust the Timing

There will be many, many times over the years that you will wonder, "Why?" *Why am I doing this? Will it ever get better? Why can't I get ahead? Will I ever get ahead? Will I ever be able to do something that completely lights me up? And how will I ever even figure out what that is? Will it ever make sense?*

Just keep following the path that is slowly being laid out for you. There will be many times when you will look back over the sequence of events and be amazed at how they all connect together. It will absolutely and totally blow your mind how the path was being laid out to bring you to where you are today. The dots will connect, and the picture of what you are meant to be doing here will be crystal clear. As the time comes to write the contribution for this book, things will come full circle and then some. An opportunity to work with the health and wellness company that you were presented with several years ago will come up again, and it all falls into place.

The lightbulb is even brighter than it was before. That first introduction to the health and wellness company opened you up to the idea of being an entrepreneur, of working for yourself, and the world of personal development. A few years later, you will be introduced to a loose-leaf tea company. Through being a "Sipologist," you will be thrown into the world of social media and online marketing — learning about Facebook, Instagram, Canva, and more. It is through searching online events on Facebook that you will come across an ad for that October 2018 workshop. This leads me to the idea of tuning into your intuition …

2. Trust Your Intuition

Listen to the little whispers that guide you on your path. Pay attention to when you are feeling the full body, "Yes, I need to do this." Your gut will never steer you wrong. Think back to that day in 2018 when you decided to attend that workshop. Something within you spoke to you and told you that this is what you needed to do that day. Over the next few years, you will be tested. You will learn to distinguish between what is a full body "yes" and what is not. Believe me, you will learn to recognize the difference. It's important to honor that. And you may be wondering, how do I even recognize when it's a "full yes" or not? The first way is to find a quiet space. Take a few deep breaths and picture yourself following your "yes" and doing whatever it is that you are considering. How does your body feel? Do you feel light and expanded? Or does your body feel tense and constricted in places? Take a moment to feel into that. Now picture yourself saying "no" to it. How does your body feel this time? What feels better in your body — saying "yes" or saying "no"?

This is exactly what you did when the opportunity to write a contribution for this book came up. *What does contributing a piece feel like in my body? And what does reading the book in the world without my contribution in it feel like?* The choice is clear. As scary as it is to think about writing a piece, you know you have to do it. But let's be real here, the fears may still come up. As you are considering writing this piece, the old questions are going to come up again. *Who am I to be writing a chapter of a book? Do I actually have anything important to say? When people read it, will they think it's any good?* But the choice is yours — who are you writing this piece for? If there's even one person who reads it and takes even one small idea or new thought from it, it will be worth it. You are worthy of sharing your story.

3. You Make it Through it All

You have far more strength than you could ever have imagined. There are going to be many, many times when you think, "How could I possibly take on any more? When will the roller coaster end? When will life just give me a break?" But you get through it. Through all the disappointments, tears, frustration, anger, hopelessness, and aimlessness. You get through it all. Not only do you get through it, but you grow in ways you never thought possible and use it all to propel you forward.

You move to a place where you want to teach others about what you have learned. You want to create programs to guide them through the focus word of the month journey so that they have new coping mechanisms and a toolbox of tricks for when times get tough for them too. Journaling, gratitude practices, meditation, and many more things that you probably haven't heard of yet are going to become part of your everyday life. Embrace it all. Take it one new idea at a time — don't try to do too much too soon.

So dear younger self, just keep going. Like I mentioned earlier, you started this Project in 2019, and early in 2020, the COVID-19 pandemic hit. It threw the world into a complete shutdown, and it forced you into a deeper period of questioning. A lot of the things we considered "normal" were taken away from us. You will keep hearing people say, "Let's just get back to normal." But this all will give you the opportunity to question what you want your "normal" to be. How do you want to take care of your health — all aspects of your health, physical, emotional, mental, and spiritual? Has the way you've been living your life actually worked for you? What aspects of it would you like to change?

As you navigate yourself through this time, things are going to be turned inside out and upside down for you. Project Worthiness will give you the strength and perseverance to keep going through all of it. In the back of your mind, the voice of Project Worthiness will get you through this.

Things will keep coming up day after day, week after week, month after month, until finally, one day, you answer the call. You say to the Universe, "Alright, I get your message. The power is within me, and it has been all the time. I have the power to completely change the course of my life." Stop getting caught up in all the "if only" and "it's too late." Just decide here and now that the time is now. You have all the pieces of the puzzle, and you know how it all fits together — offer the mindset programs with the support of the health and wellness products. Just simply step in and do the thing. Project Worthiness: A Year to Discover and Empower Myself has now evolved into Project Worthiness: Mind, Body and Soul Activation.

And what exactly does that all mean? It means supporting the mind and body in every way possible so that your soul's vision and mission can come alive — so that your true self and soul can shine brightly. And finally, as you are closing out the chapter in what will be the first of many writing projects, always remember to be the light that you know you were meant to be here.

You are worthy. You have always been worthy, and you always will be worthy.

About Michelle Millson

Michelle Millson was born in Winnipeg, Manitoba and now lives in Woodstock, Ontario, Canada, with her husband and four cats.

While her educational background includes child development psychology and Montessori teacher training, she has worked primarily in the retail, customer service, and office admin fields.

In 2010, she was introduced to the world of network marketing through USANA Health Sciences. She pairs the health and wellness products from USANA and the loose-leaf teas from Sipology by Steeped Tea with her mindset and empowerment journal prompts to create Project Worthiness: Mind, Body and Soul activation.

Project Worthiness is primarily seen on Instagram as a series of journal prompts and activity recommendations surrounding a theme word for each month. Michelle has created a journal and has plans to create more journals or eBooks around the CARE principles — Creativity, Authenticity, Resiliency, and Elevation.

It is through the exploration of these words that the foundation is built for further self-development and growth. These four words tie into the four key areas of health — physical, mental, emotional, and social.

Through these word explorations and the health and wellness products, the mind and body can be properly supported so the soul's mission and vision can come alive.

For more information — Linktr.ee//Project_Worthiness

The Power of No

I can feel a knot in my stomach from reading that title. Just the *thought* of saying "no" to someone makes me feel tense, anxious, and deeply uncomfortable. *Won't that create tension? Will they think I'm difficult or stop liking me? Isn't it just easier to say "yes" and keep everyone happy?*

If you feel the same, it's likely that you, like me, have people-pleasing tendencies.

One of the problems with people-pleasing (constantly putting the needs of others before your own, acting to keep others happy rather than on your own wants or needs) is that it's exhausting. Constantly expending energy to meet others' needs at the expense of your own is a thankless task, especially as we ultimately cannot provide others' happiness. Happiness comes from within.

My personal blend of people-pleasing is less about people liking me (although that would be nice too!) and more about avoiding tension or conflict and/or being perceived as "difficult." I grew up with food allergies at a time when they weren't very prevalent and spent my childhood feeling awkward that others were having to accommodate me and my needs, particularly when I could tell it was causing them some trouble.

This has manifested in a whole host of ways, including:
- going with what I anticipated others wanted, rather than what I wanted
- doing what was expected to avoid getting in trouble
- saying "yes"/avoiding saying "no" when I was asked to do something, even if it caused me inconvenience or hardship

"No" has not been a comfortable word in my vocabulary. It is such an emotionally charged word, especially for some women, I sense. And women are more likely to have people-pleasing tendencies, perhaps because of the caring, nurturing roles we have traditionally had in society. We want everyone to be ok; we want people to like us and think well of us; we feel pressure to do the "shoulds" and "must dos." But when we are always giving, focusing our attention on everyone else's wellbeing, and we have no boundaries, our energy becomes depleted. We end up giving from a place of deficiency, running on empty, feeling tense, and living in our heads. It can cause feelings of resentment towards the people we are giving our energy to and frustration and bitterness that we have no time for ourselves. People-pleasers are usually disconnected from our higher selves and our true purpose here on earth. By focusing all our attention on others' needs, there is no space, time, or energy to excavate our light, claim our purpose in this life and allow our souls to shine. As a people-pleaser, the hardest and most important lesson is to learn to get comfortable with "no."

When we say "no" and set boundaries, we are prioritizing ourselves. We stop giving our energy away and create space for nourishment and transformation. We allow energy in and make space for something new. We can reconnect to our higher selves, to the Universe; we can tap into wells of creative energy and unearth our light and our true purpose in life and then share that with the world.

Even now, the thought of getting comfortable with saying "no" creates tension in my body. It's too awkward, too difficult, too painful. What will people think of me? Will it create conflict? The thought of saying "no" from this perspective seems sharp and like a slap in the face. And this is totally understandable when "no" is presented as a dichotomy: *yes OR no*, or as an absolute: *No means no*.

But what if it isn't either of those things? What if it's:

"No, thank you." "No more." "*Not* today."

What if we view "yes" and "no" as degrees or a gradient? "No" then becomes a spectrum from "not at all" to "no more," framing it in a new context and creating many new possibilities. I can't promise that reframing "no" in this way will instantly make it a comfortable word in your vocabulary or that overnight, you'll become a dab hand at setting healthy boundaries, but it's *not* a bad start (see what I did there?!).

It's not only saying "no" to others that can feel like scary territory. It can be challenging to set healthy boundaries for ourselves. What if I say "no" to doing the housework/things that are expected of me/old patterns of behavior so I can focus on the things that really bring me joy? Does that mean the "shoulds" will never be done, or I'm going to have to do them anyway, just when I'm feeling more tired? Do I always have to get all my tasks, jobs, and "should dos" done before I can sit down to enjoy reading my book, begin a creative endeavor, or (Heaven forbid) rest?

I urge you to experiment and find out. If all else fails, you can always go back to the old ways. But something better might happen (and it usually does). I've been playing with this idea recently and challenging myself to do the thing that I really want to first and to move all the "shoulds" (and even some of the "must dos") further down the list. It can feel really uncomfortable to start with, but I always tell myself that I can always go back to the old ways and that nothing will change unless I try something new. So far, I've found that, on the days where I prioritize the things that make me feel good, I am generally more focused and more productive, have greater energy, and a better frame of mind. I feel a deeper sense of connection to my higher self and better understand my life purpose and what I'm really here to do in the world. I feel powerful. I shine.

And guess what — the world keeps turning, and I've learned that the "shoulds," and even some of the "must-dos," can actually wait for a while.

It's ok to start small when learning to become comfortable with saying "no." This will be different for everyone, so I urge you to experiment. What if we allow ourselves to say "no" to something that will be draining and exhausting? How about saying "yes" to that but "no" to that? What if we say "no" to letting fears stop us? Or start with saying "no" to some of the old rules that we've put in place for ourselves?

It can be an uncomfortable and bumpy ride at first, but it's also empowering and liberating. Saying "no" in the context of setting healthy boundaries and putting our own needs first is creating space for our soul light to shine. This has been one of the biggest revelations to me (and believe me, I'm still on this journey!): *If I am saying "no" to that, I am saying "yes" to something else. Creating space for possibilities.*

The first "no" I've been experimenting with is saying "no" to pushing myself in any context. I've become very accustomed to digging deep, gritting my teeth, and pushing myself to start a task, finish a chore or tick one more job off the list. I feel the pressure to get things done, and tasks of almost any kind can feel as if they're hanging over me. Even things I really want to do, like writing my book or tending to my allotment, can feel draining when they become "shoulds," and I push myself to do them. Pushing feels tense, depleting, exhausting, and puts me very much in my head, so I'm saying "*no*" to that and in setting that boundary, again and again, I'm creating space to *feel* into what I really want to do (instead of what my head tells me I "should" do) and giving myself permission to do it. This approach (which I call "allowing") feels relaxed, nourishing, gets me out of my head, and reconnected to how I feel. I find it energizes me, like I tap into wells of energy and creativity that weren't accessible to me when I was pushing. I feel plugged back in to the Universe and become clear on what I'm here in this life to do: I reconnect to my life's purpose. For me, that's about bringing light to the world, and my light shines more brightly when I stop pushing and start allowing.

This is still a work in progress for me, but setting boundaries is like exercising a muscle, which becomes stronger over time and then requires less effort. The more you do it, the less thought it requires, the less concerted effort is needed; it becomes habitual. This is not to say that setting boundaries is always easy, but it becomes a more familiar road.

By working on saying "no" and setting boundaries with myself, I've also become more aware of the need to set them with other people and in other contexts. Until recently, I can't remember ever saying "no" to anything I was asked to do at work. I have always given everything to my job and said "yes" to whatever I've been asked. "No" has never seemed like an option. It's only reflecting back now that I can see that this has required me to dig deep and constantly push. *For years.* It has been energetically depleting and mentally exhausting, and I can see now that giving all my reserves of energy in this way has suffocated my soul, taken me away from living my life's purpose, and significantly dimmed my light.

I recently said "no" for the first time, or rather my body said it for me. I was in a difficult meeting, being asked to take on yet another huge project with a tight deadline, and I burst into tears. Something that has never happened in my ten years of being with this company or at any time in my working life. When discussing with my manager afterward, I realized I could not be pushed any further. I felt, in my soul, that I could give no more. This "no" was not going to become a "yes." I had just set a boundary.

I felt uncomfortable and vulnerable and, at the same time, liberated and exhilarated. And unbelievably (so it seemed to me at the time), that boundary was accepted and respected. In that moment, I became someone who has boundaries. Of course, it wasn't all resolved in that one discussion, but "no" has finally joined my work vocabulary and opened up possibilities for so much transformation, both in my current role and also in my life more widely. I realized I was saying "no" to working in a state of deple- tion, with all my energy and creativity being used for something that is not in line with my life's purpose; so, what was I saying "yes" to?

I've had to take some time to reflect on this question and to get to know (and set) my boundaries, which is a constant and ongoing process. As a result, I am creating a life that feels much more closely aligned to my life purpose, and I know that this journey will continue. I feel empowered, energized, and like I am fully claiming my purpose for the first time ever. I am writing a book on the transformational power of self-kindness (within which healthy boundaries play a key role) and training to be a forest bathing guide, two endeavors that definitely enable me to shine. I am continuing to say "no" to pushing and "yes" to allowing, and although still in the same employment, it no longer saps my energy in the same way. I know where my boundaries are and check in with them regularly, and this is key. Boundaries are rarely a one-and-done activity. They are constantly tested, shaped, and developed. What may be an enthusiastic "yes" on one day may be a firm "no" on the next. The key is to keep checking in with ourselves and our boundaries as often as possible. The power of saying "no" to something is that we are saying "yes" to something else. Lots of (big or little) "nos" in a day can create space to come back to ourselves, get back into alignment, and let our souls shine.

About Holly Yandall

Holly Yandall is an author living on the south coast of England. She is currently writing a book about the power of self-kindness to change the world, sharing how, by getting out of our heads and reconnecting with nature, we can heal ourselves and the planet.

Holly is happiest outdoors: walking by the sea with her husband and dogs, pottering on her allotment, or running with friends.

A passionate advocate for spending time in nature, Holly is training to be a forest bathing guide.

You can follow Holly's writing journey on Instagram @selfkindtribe

Remember Why You Came

I didn't know I was sleeping, that my light had dimmed, that my soul had lost its shine. I thought I was doing it "right." I got a degree, got married, and had a home and a good job. I had the kids; why wasn't I happy? Why did I feel so restless? Why didn't things feel "right" if I was following the path everyone said I should? Why was I lashing out, feeling so angry and sad?

Life was supposed to be more beautiful than this, and I knew it. My body and soul knew, too, and they were trying to send me messages, but my mind was still trying to rationalize it all. My mind would tell me that something must be wrong with me or that I must be doing it wrong, but my soul knew there was more to the story.

So, I started the excavation and healing journey I am still on today because, as I now know, healing is not linear. I found a therapist and began my work unraveling things I didn't know were there inside of me. Beliefs, trauma, and fear that I didn't know I carried for both myself and mostly for others. I realized I had been unconsciously conditioned to be co-dependent. Mix that with being a deeply feeling empath, and it was the perfect storm. I had no idea what was mine and what wasn't.

The Unraveling

Motherhood was my first awakening to figuring this out. It showed me why I felt triggered almost all the time by my kids and didn't have the tools to work through it or help them develop their own sense of self and emotional awareness. It was not the story of motherhood I had longed for, and yet I felt so powerless to change it. I realized I was getting ready to pass on all the trauma from my ancestral line plus my own shit that I had been carrying to them, and my soul was saying, "Enough; it stops with you." In hindsight, the message was loud and clear. "Chase your own healing, not just for you, but for them."

So, I leaned in even more deeply. I started to become more curious. I started listening to my own wild wisdom within and began listening to the questions it was asking. I started to realize something within my marriage was very wrong and had been for quite some time. Why weren't we connecting? Was this just how it was supposed to be in a long-term partnership? Where was the desire, where was the passion? Had we lost it? Was it porn, lack of desire — what was going on? My partner of 12 years at the time denied anything was wrong. I started to feel like maybe I was just crazy or paranoid. And then one random night in January of 2019, in a bathroom that wasn't even mine, while our two beautiful daughters slept peacefully in the next room, it all came tumbling out. Like a river washing over me, both suffocating and freeing at the same time, the words he spoke, "I had an affair," came bubbling out.

These were words I never thought I would hear. The level of betrayal I felt was smothering at first. Then with reflection, gut-wrenching grief at times, and more therapy, I began to let it burn a raging fire within me. I let it burn all the narratives, beliefs, and fears that had been keeping me small. I saw my true soul for the first time and how beautiful and radiant she truly was. How she deserved to be cherished, nurtured, and loved. How she had dreams all her own and her own magic and medicine within. She called me into my own healing through one of the darkest, most uncertain times of my life. She helped me find my light. She connected me back to my soul shine.

The Journey Continues

As many days have passed since that initial fire was lit inside me, and much of the old has burned away, I have realized it was only just the beginning of learning how to bloom wildly and listen to the call of my own soul. Healing has come in many layers for me. It is a practice of continuing to return to the sacred. To continue to remember why I came here in this lifetime. To stay grounded and connected to the things that root me in my own truth.

Here is what I am learning so far about the journey of healing and a process to help you in your own journey, should you so choose.

Step 1: First, you feel. You feel very real feelings. The energy in motion within you. Let it move in and through while knowing you aren't those feelings. Your essence is not what happened to you. Your essence is your own compass, the magic of your soul. The suffering happens when you become disconnected from it. You never lost it, but you do have to mindfully plug back in.

Step 2: Learn your own patterns and triggers and stop feeding into them. Bring them to conscious light and stop giving yourself over to them.

Step 3: Redirect your energy to the sacred — to your sacred wellbeing. Call upon your guides — the Goddess, God, Mother Earth, Source — and root in them. Reconnect to your life force, your creativity, and your innovation. The more you do this, you write a new story for yourself. You move out of indoctrination. You stop cock-blocking your magic. You stop the self-sabotage.

Step 4: You do this through your sacred wellness practices. This is beyond clichéd "self-care." This is the non-negotiable wellness of your soul. The lighthouse for your body, mind, and spirit. The energy source for all of your being. When you look at these practices as non-negotiables, you see them in a different light.

Step 5: You understand the complete importance of breaking and completing the cycle all in one. You commit to never forsaking yourself again and knowing your own worth. You practice radical acts of self-love and care daily. You are deserving of the most true and beautiful life, and it's up to you to call that in, embody it, and illuminate anything that does not respect it physically or energetically.

That is the call of Your Wild Soul.

Reminder, you are a sovereign being, not a victim of your circumstances.

Your Wild Soul

My wild soul is calling me to continue to illuminate my own healing journey and story so that I can create safe and sacred spaces for others to do the same. I realize that my mess is my message, and it is calling me deeper and deeper into disrupting the current paradigms we find ourselves in. I can create a new way of being in this lifetime and help facilitate healing for others, especially women.

It is my deepest belief in all of my healing work thus far that we all possess our own magic and medicine. We all have what we need already inside us to heal and live the most true and beautiful life meant for us. We weren't meant to live an existence of suffering; we were truly meant to shine and radiate from the essence of who we are, our soul.

You are invited into your own soul journey. What is your wild soul calling you to? How is she wanting to shine? You may not know, and that is ok. Sit with it. Create some space for it. Listen to your own nudges. Let your wild wisdom lead you. It can feel scary as hell at first but keep honoring it. It is your own internal compass here to align you with your most true and beautiful life. The one you are already worthy of. The one you don't have to strive or hustle for. When you are willing to slow down, listen deeply, release the petals of the things no longer serving you, and root in your own sacred wellness, then and only then can you bloom wildly and live in your fullest expression.

This world needs our fullest expression. We are being called back to our wholeness and to stop cutting off parts of ourselves to make others comfortable. It's time to let ourselves be fully seen, known, and loved. This will allow us to retrieve the sacred feminine and heal the masculine within each of us. Can you feel it? We are the leaders this world is waiting for. Will we answer the call? Will we allow our souls to shine?

I'm in. Are you?

About Katie May

Katie May is a soul coach, healing facilitator, and Wild Mother Goddess who believes in creating her own magic. She has worked as a nurse for 16 years in the specialty of palliative care and hospice, supporting those at the end of life's journey as an RN and clinical nurse specialist. Through this work, she was inspired to help people live in the most connected and healed way possible. She discovered her love for whole health, soul care, and spiritual mentorship and now is an inspiring coach and mentor who creates safe and sacred spaces for people to reconnect with and embrace their own magic and medicine within so they can live in reverence to their own internal seasons and live in full bloom. Katie is married to her partner, and they live in the mountains of North Carolina with their two children. She is always up for an adventure and finding ways to connect more deeply with the greatest Mother of all, Mother Earth.

To check out more of her work and offerings, or to connect with Katie, you can find her through her website www.embraceyourselfwhole.com

Turning to the Light

In April 2019, my best friend, Jen, and I got together to plan our next step in life. We were both nearing 40 and felt we weren't living the lives we wanted. So, we asked each other, "What would you do if you knew you could never fail?" I couldn't help it; my inner child came out and said, "I'd be on stage singing and acting — I'd be in a musical!"

Jen turned to me, looked me straight in the eye, and said, "Jody, my goal for you would be not to give a fuck what people think."

I knew she was right, but I also knew that I hadn't always been like this. I would need a massive dose of self-belief and self-worth to be that person again.

It took another five months before I did anything about Jen's words, and it started with a job change.

I'd been working at the same place for 17 years; things were stagnant, and I was miserable. I had no personal goals or desires, I didn't think I was worthy of having them, and I certainly didn't know I was allowed them. So, to overcome this total funk, I'd applied for a different position in another department, hoping it would be just the thing to kick start my career, motivation, and life.

It didn't.

I didn't get the job, and my original role no longer existed. After 17 years, I was facing redundancy.

Eventually, I accepted it and walked away with a neat little package that would last for about ten months.

Then it struck me, what do you do when you're about to turn 40, your kids are getting older, all your experience is in one industry, and you no longer want to work in that industry anymore?

It was both exhilarating and scary. You know when someone says the world is your oyster? That's what it felt like, so many options and possibilities, but I had no idea what I wanted to do. I was overwhelmed and lost because my whole identity was in that role, and it was also where all my confidence, self-belief, and self-worth had been ground down over the last few years. As a result, I was a complete shell of who I used to be. In fact, I didn't recognize who I used to be or who I was now.

I spent the next three months numb and in a complete daze, but despite that, I got a part-time job as an admin assistant. I didn't need to; I took it because I was worried the money would run out. It wouldn't. That was just the scarcity mindset I was in.

The part-time job was ok, but I dreaded going in after a few weeks. It didn't light me up, it wasn't challenging me, and the business itself was 20 years out of date, including the people that worked there.

Within three months of starting there, the redundancy finally hit me, and I had a breakdown. I went to the doctors and referred myself to a therapist.

I always thought grief was reserved for deaths, but I realized during therapy that grief can happen for any loss, even a job loss. And when you've put your life, heart, and soul into a business and built your entire identity around it for 17 years, to wake up one day and no longer a part of it, that's a significant loss.

I was grieving for the loss of structure, the routine, the belonging and most of all, I was grieving for losing me. Because it was during this time that I realized how small I'd made myself. I wanted so badly to fit in that I changed who I was, I became quieter, and my people-pleasing tendencies were on overdrive. I didn't want to be seen, yet I wanted to be seen — confusing, right?

While working with my therapist, I journaled every day to help process my feelings and thoughts and rebuild myself. I started looking into spirituality and saving as many positive affirmations as possible on my phone. And one stuck with me; it said,

"Some people are going to reject you simply because your light shines too bright for them. That's ok; keep shining!"

I realized then that was me, but instead of continuing to shine my light, I'd switched mine off completely. I couldn't remember the last time it was on. There was a flicker of it in the new job when I could see how much I could improve processes and systems or make suggestions to improve customer service, but whenever I did this and felt I was starting to flicker, someone would frown at me, act differently towards me, make me feel like I didn't belong or look at me as if to say, "Who does she think she is?"

So, I switched it down again, but I kept repeating that quote because something had shifted. The affirmations and the therapy were starting to work. My spirituality was growing. I absolutely loved the spiritual world I was entering. I would consume all I could on the power of positive affirmations, finding your joy, the moon, the power of nature's cycles, using oracle cards to guide my way, and so much more.

A new world was opening up for me, and I wanted more. I could feel myself lighting up again.

I began to realize and believe I was better than the part-time job I was in. I knew it was killing my soul slowly and that if I didn't get out, I could be stuck there for another 17 years. But still, the fear was holding me back from making any moves; then, in March 2020, the world changed.

The U.K. went into lockdown, and five months after the redundancy, I was furloughed.

This was the pause I needed. The pause I needed to grieve, explore, and heal.

I journaled every day in my garden before the house woke and home-schooling started. I took my kids for walks along the canal and over the fields almost daily. I was reconnecting with myself and nature.

It felt incredible. I wanted more. I deserved more.

Then ten months after my redundancy, I faced redundancy again. But this time, I felt free, and I wasn't scared.

I spent the next few months exploring ideas for businesses. Even though the admin job had been soul-destroying, it made me realize how much knowledge I had about running a business, how many skills I had that were transferable and that I didn't want to spend the second part of my life throwing my mind, body, and soul into someone else's dream. I wanted my own.

So, in September 2020, almost a year after the first redundancy, I set up my own virtual assistant business — basically, admin support for small business owners. But the big difference was I could choose whom I worked with and what type of work I wanted to do.

It sounds incredible, right? But it didn't come without its struggles. My light might have been shining more brightly, but so were my people-pleasing tendencies. And I never considered I would have to overcome issues with boundaries, but that's another story for another day.

So, there I was, my light shining brighter. I knew my worth. I knew I had many skills, lots of knowledge, and life and career experience to bring to any table. And I did it — my VA client base slowly built up, and I had a steady income stream. But my light wasn't fully shining; something was missing.

It was my joy. The thing that lights me up. The thing that excites me.

Then, one day I came across Reiki. As soon as I read about it, I knew it was for me. The idea that we can heal ourselves and others with universal energy felt exciting. I wanted to know more, and I wanted to experience it myself. So, in January 2021, I signed up for Reiki level one and absolutely loved it; it helped me on so many levels. And four months later, I trained for level two and became a Reiki practitioner. Then in May 2022, I became a Reiki master teacher.

I'd found it. I'd found the thing that would light me up.

So, I took what gave me the most joy — Reiki, spirituality, healing and helping people — and created a second business, Spiritual Wellness. But had I fully healed? Was my light shining fully?

The thing with healing is that you may feel you've healed, but it's not until other people start to notice that you believe you have. I knew I felt different; I felt like my light wasn't just flickering. It was on full beam, but could other people see it?

Then one day, my question was answered when my friend Jo tagged me in a post, showing this poem:

The Flower by Chelan Harkin Poetry
The flower never had a to-do list, not one day of her life.
She just pointed her whole self toward the light.
The rest took care of itself.

Jo and I met in 2020, and Jo's witnessed my journey from redundancy to first-time VA business owner to dual business owner and Reiki master. On the tag, Jo wrote, "Jody, this made me think of you."

When I saw those words, my heart burst with pride as I realized how far I'd come; I felt I was lighting up by turning to the light. When you turn to the light, you have to be a little bit brave, a little bit courageous, and a little bit "I don't give two f**ks what you think of me." Especially if you've had your light dimmed like me.

And the tricky thing with having your light dimmed is you don't know it's happened until one day you wake up and realize you're not doing the thing that brings you joy. You're not standing up for yourself. Instead, you spend most of your time and energy trying to keep other people happy. Constantly worrying about what other people think. Not putting your ideas or opinions forward because you believe they don't matter.

Sound familiar?

The other sneaky thing about light dimming is finding out when it first started; it could have started in childhood with comments from adults like, "Be a good girl" (please everyone but yourself), "Children must be seen and not heard" (don't stand out), "Do as you're told" (you don't have a say), "Don't show off" (don't be proud of your achievements), "Stop being silly" (don't have fun).

When I was 10, I was dancing at a family wedding. I remember an adult glancing at me curiously and then whispering to another adult; that was enough to stop me right there in my tracks. It's subtle. Just like the comments from the people in my very last office job.

And because it's subtle, we don't notice, and over the years, it becomes ingrained and the "norm." We don't question why we're the way we are; our friends and family accept us; they know us as us. So, we just go with it until we reach a certain age or experience a significant change in our life. For me, it was redundancy. But it could be an illness, having children, a death, menopause, or reading this book.

But when you do notice, it's like a veil is lifted. It's scary, overwhelming, frustrating, and regretful. But it's also exciting, expansive, joyful, and freeing, knowing you can finally see clearly and be who you want to be.

You might need inner-child healing, Reiki, NLP, or therapy to be able to turn your light back on. And it will be hard, but it's so worth it.

But if you're brave enough to walk the path and do uncover the moments when your light was dimmed, here are some things to remember.

- Look into your past but don't dwell there.
- Find a trusted mentor to work through them.
- Find a trusted therapist if you feel you need professional help.
- Journal, journal, journal; the power of writing down your thoughts and feelings is such a good healing tool.
- Talk to others about your experiences; when we share, the healing starts.
- Find your joy.

Be like all the authors in this book.

Be The Flower from the poem.

Point yourself to the light and let your light reflect on others to give them the self-belief, courage, bravery, and strength to do the same.

And if all that fails, just remember my friend Jen's advice: "Don't give a fuck about what anyone thinks."

About Jody Woodbridge

Jody has been on a path of self-discovery since accepting redundancy in 2019 from a management role. In 2021, she found her calling as a Reiki master and self-care alchemist and founded Spiritual Wellness: A Place to Heal, Connect, Share and Practice Self-Care.

Jody believes everyone should and can have access to Reiki. She explains, *"(Reiki) it's helped me on many levels. It's given me a sense of peace and an understanding of myself. Through Reiki and Spiritual Wellness, I am calmer, and I've developed a deeper connection to nature, her cycles and the energy around me. It's allowed me to tune in and align myself with these cycles, bringing me back into balance. By understanding and practicing self-healing, I've realized the importance of taking the time and creating space for self-care. I want to spread the word about the magic of Reiki and the importance of taking time for ourselves."*

Jody has a membership where you learn how to practice self-care, receive Reiki, and work in tune with nature and the moon cycles. She holds Menopause Healing Support groups, created a Self-Care program, and wants to bring Reiki into the workplace with her Workplace Wellbeing Reiki packages.

She's based in Cheshire, U.K., is a mum of two boys (11 and 13), and a wife to Pete; she enjoys walks in nature, journaling and open water swimming (as long as it isn't too cold!).

"I believe energy is everything and everywhere; when we know and understand this, anything is possible."

www.spiritualwellness.uk

Shine Your Soul Even When You Are Judged or Hurt, Don't Dim Your Light

Have you ever been hurt by a group of "mean girls" or excluded from a group and not invited? Have you ever learned that a woman you trusted had been gossiping about you?

Was there ever a time they had your back on social media but didn't have your back offline?

Do you have a ***soul-sister scar*** from a betrayal from girlfriends, sisters, your mom, business partner, corporate businesswoman, or female peers where you had to dim your light while you were judged for something you did or said that was not your intention?

Maybe it was as a child, in high school, college, or even as an adult? Your soul's light shined too bright for them, and so you had to tone it down. I have a soul scar from a yoga mentor who led from ego. She was not clear in her intentions when she offered to help me as a new yoga studio owner.

We, as humans, naturally judge ourselves and others. We must take our power back and retrain our minds and hearts to not judge ourselves and others. We must learn to accept ourselves unconditionally so we can love others unconditionally! We learn to radically accept ourselves!

I find myself still sometimes triggered when this **soul scar scab** gets ripped off wide open from the traumatic experience of being hurt by another woman whom I trusted. I am grateful that over the past ten years, I've been able to develop self-awareness, yoga psychology, breathwork, meditation, mindfulness, emotional regulation, Somatic Mind-Body Yoga Therapy, emotional rinsing, divine faith, and prayer skills to process my emotions when they now surface.

Through this painful life experience, I have practiced not projecting hurt onto others but rather using these skills such as journaling, yoga, breathwork, and emotional rinsing that will process hurt, anger, resentment, sadness, depression, fear, grief, and other difficult emotions in a healthy way vs. projecting it back onto others.

As an empath and a very sensitive little girl growing up into a highly sensitive woman with a wounded inner child, I have experienced being bullied and excluded — including in high school, at college within my sorority, and in adult life. As a child, I used to bring hurt birds home to my dad and ask him, "Fix it, Daddy." This was who I was at my core. My soul and my authentic self were — and are — loving, compassionate, empathic, and sensitive. The years of hurt and human disappointment forced me to wear many masks to survive and dull my shine. For more than 15 years in the corporate world dominated by males, I was left with a constant feeling of needing to protect myself. I would learn later in life that this was a trauma response.

Hurt people will hurt people unless they heal their generational trauma and wounds. Many of us walk around the planet unconscious of the projections we are putting onto others. We are each simply holding up a sacred mirror for each other in the healing journey. Our healing journeys are lifelong processes of growth, and life lessons always present themselves. We open ourselves up to a beginner's mind, a mindfulness concept, and being lifelong students. We can see the world as a place of having our back and working for us, not against us. We will see the world and life experiences through a different lens of consciousness, compassion, love, non-judgment, radical acceptance, and self-awareness.

After coming off this very traumatic experience earlier in 2017, it opened up a beautiful healing opportunity I discovered in spring 2017 in Los Angeles, CA — Venice Beach. This was at the beginning of my transformational yoga psychology teacher training immersion healing journey. This lesson would deepen my life's unique dharma, my soul's purpose, to heal so that I could *shine my soul's light* into the world.

As a **wounded healer**, when our soul's calling is to help others heal, first, we must heal ourselves more deeply. We can only take others through what we have authentically experienced ourselves. Family of origin and shadow soul work is essential to be able to fully *shine our soul* by healing intergenerational trauma. It was in 2017 that I discovered my family of origin inner work. We must release the samskara (thought, emotion, behavior) patterns based on our trauma and family of origin so we can live the highest calling in our lives and version of ourselves.

It was May 2018 in Los Angeles, California. I had flown across the country to be part of this training! I was going deeper into my journey, focusing on the family of origin lineage generational healing, and inner shadow soul work. It had taken over 20 years of talk therapy, group and individual Cognitive Behavior Therapy (CBT), and self-help books until I was ready for the **yoga psychology deep work.** Having a background of four generations of physical, emotional, and verbal abuse in my family of origin on my dad's side, I was in my 40s by the time I got into the deep healing work that would change my life's work trajectory.

Growing outside my comfort zone in the depths of an in-person yoga psychology teacher training immersion. I stood in a **sacred soul healing circle** in the middle of a group of 30 women witnessing and supporting me. I was held, safe, and not judged. I was wearing batting gloves, holding a padded bat, with a pile of yoga blankets and bolsters in front of me. As our group leader rang the yoga tingsha bells three times to start the ceremony and sacred practice, I was preparing myself to do an emotional rinsing session, not knowing what would come out. It was a raw, instinctive, animal-like experience when you completely surrender and are vulnerable to **let go** of control and surrender to what comes to the surface.

As I started hitting the blankets, tears of the release of hurt feelings, disappointment, abandonment, and betrayal came streaming down my face. There was no rage, only deep sadness under the anger iceberg. It was so instinctive as my body, mind, and breath started to flow. Emotion is energy in motion; what was dormant in the subconscious mind and stored in my body was coming out **full force.** I remember crying, yelling, pausing, and talking to this yoga psychology therapist mentor, hitting the blankets over and over until I was exhausted. Instead of supporting me, my very first yoga mentor became jealous that I had started a yoga studio and yoga teacher training program early in my career, and she had not in her 30 years.

I can remember saying, "How could you do that to me?" "You were supposed to be my yoga mentor!" "I trusted you!" Coming from the corporate world, yoga was supposed to be a place of emotional safety. I could see looking back she had her own insecurity and unhealed wounds that she was projecting onto me. She had a lack of self-confidence and a true sense of worth seeking validation from those around her versus true self-love and acceptance. She was also operating from a sense of ego and a lack of self-awareness of how her words and actions were affecting me and those around her, including the entire group.

In my mind, I thought I had forgiven her, but clearly, this betrayal trauma had stayed in my body and needed to be released. I remember feeling shocked that this was coming out of my body. What I was most grateful for was the testimony of this rinsing technique working. As I interacted with her through the yoga community indirectly, I was no longer viscerally triggered by her name or the sight of her Facebook posts anymore. It gave me **freedom**. I had taken my **power and my peace back** that I had given away to her.

I am a firm believer that there is a lesson in everything that happens for us, not to us. There's always something good that comes out of even the most painful experiences turning pain into purpose. Our wounds are our wisdom. This experience inspired me to help other students and teachers shine their soul through this rinsing and yoga psychology inner work. I brought this rinsing experience back with me from Los Angeles to Raleigh, North Carolina, as well as online globally and still teach it to this day. It helps people around the world in releasing what is not serving them and creating blockages of living their life's purpose. This experience inspired me in 2017 to begin working one on one and in groups offering rinsing and other yoga psychology coaching healing modalities.

I remember the sense of relief after I was witnessed in front of that group of women. How powerful and grateful I was for that sense of support. Little did I know at the time that it would be an inspiration to want to support other women in their healing journey and yoga careers in the future.

I remember the sense of **kula**, soul sisterhood, in yoga psychology we created with these women. *Kula* is a Sanskrit word that can be translated as **"community," "clan," or "tribe."** This word is used by the yoga community to define the sense of inclusion and belonging that can be cultivated through yogis coming together to practice yoga, meditation, or prayer. To be fully seen, heard, validated, and supported versus being in an environment of competition, ego, jealousy, and envy.

I sat back and listened to other strong women who were also on their own individual healing journeys full of trauma and difficult life experiences. I was so grateful to be in the presence of such a powerful, strong group of women. There was much inspiration for me to take this same feeling out into the world and have other women feel this sense of support and inclusion.

Looking back, I see that my light shined too bright for my original yoga mentor. I definitely felt a sense of needing to "dim my light" as she had stopped growing as a teacher after 30-plus years. She was focused on ego and "knowing" everything about yoga versus living her yoga off the mat and staying a lifelong student. She was focused on the competition, keeping the attention on her, rather than lifting up other women.

For many teachers, this type of traumatic experience would have stopped them in their tracks! They would not have continued as a yoga teacher or in yoga service. I knew another yoga soul sister who shared a studio partnership. She came back from a week's vacation to find that all of her stuff was removed from the studio, and her partner had opened a studio down the street. She could not practice yoga for a few years as she equated it to this trauma.

I am grateful this taught me the perseverance to continue even with this obstacle and many more as I lived my yogic path of dharma, living in divine purpose from 2013 to today.

Forgiveness is a word that comes to mind as a life lesson. This experience of forgiveness allowed me to shine my soul! I had to release that deep-seated hurt, betrayal, and disappointment so I could continue to be a source of light for other students.

If we transmute our pain into purpose, instead of being bitter, we are better, we are stronger, and we can shine our soul's light brightly on those around us!

I remember a beautiful yoga soul sister, Cyndi, back in 2014. I will never forget her kind words during yoga teacher training. She said, "You were born to be a yoga teacher!" Cyndi has been an inspiration to me over the years as a soul sister and present-day who truly lifts other women up and has no jealousy, competition, or comparison — only love. A beautiful soul that truly believes, as I do, that by making others shine, we don't dim our own light. We only become a brighter beacon to inspire others to step into their calling and live their dharma in yoga — their life's purpose. Cyndi is the same behind the scenes as she posts in public, and she has my back!

Emotional rinsing is a nontraditional form of somatic mind-body yoga therapy. Our past repressed emotions and unhealed wounds remain in the mind, body, and soul and will manifest in some way if they are not released. It could show up in the form of mental health challenges such as depression, anxiety, or insomnia, which I have struggled with in the past. It will also show up in the physical body through forms such as cancer or autoimmune diseases (I also struggle with an autoimmune manifestation of unprocessed emotion stuck in the body).

Yoga became a lifesaver for me in 2013 when I went from burnout to breakdown to breakthrough. I had anxiety, depression, insomnia, was spiritually broken, and soul seeking a purpose-driven life. Already on sleeping pills for the first time in my life, waking up four times nightly, a counselor recommended yoga when anxiety meditation made me feel as if I was living outside myself. I remember when the tears kept coming and would not stop. At that moment, my therapist asked me if I needed to go to a mental health facility. I was able to get my emotions enough together to work through it with therapy and yoga. This would be the inspiration that propelled me into a yoga teacher training program after only three months of taking yoga. In less than a year, I was teaching groups of

100 students. I was *shining my soul* and remembering that purpose-driven life transition as a happy memory in my life story.

Being that part of my life's story was living a life that was not purpose-filled, when I was finally able to step into my calling, I was inspired to want to help others do the same. One of my gifts is to encourage others, to lift them up, to give them hope and unconditional love! WiseMind Soul Warrior we teach Soul Seek, Soul Heal our Soul Scars, Soul Work, Soul Care, and Soul Sister community.

God sees our intentions, our soul, our thoughts, and our emotions, and he knows everything before it happens. He's the only one who can fully heal our wounds, in addition to each of us as women being empowered to do the hard inner work! This is the only way to show up as the fully authentic version of ourselves with the outer results to let our souls shine! So, we can live our soul's calling. Listen to the calling of your soul and pay attention to what your soul is seeking to share while serving others!

I invite you to release what is no longer serving you and expand your soul so that it can shine fully. I invite you to step into a legacy of peace. I invite you to step into your Soul Seeking and calling. I invite you to do the deep inner soul healing work of our soul scars. I invite you to practice soul care. I invite you into our sacred soul sisterhood community and shine your soul!

Sending much love and light!

In service and gratitude,
Jennie Wise MHS Yogalogist
CEO WiseMind Yoga Psychology School

About Jennie Wise, Yogalogist

I've had a loud, irate inner critic my whole life! During the past ten years, I've applied my specialist training to my life. I've discovered and developed tools and techniques that help students disempower their inner critics, boost their self-worth, heal intergenerational trauma, and encourage them to believe in themselves while owning their power.

Burnout, anxiety, depression, insomnia, stress habit, inner critic, and many other patterns are what brought me to the mat. So, I've been there … I've practiced, embodied, and taught yoga for holistic mental health and transformation.

I'm a Yoga Psychology Neuroscience + Cognitive Behavior Medicine + Meditation + Trauma-Sensitive + Mindfulness transformation teacher and coach with advanced training in Los Angeles, California, shared with over 10,000 students over ten years. Completed Master of Health Science (MHS) Behavior Change, Nutrition, Disease Prevention, a published thesis.

I'm the founder and CEO of WiseMind Soul Warrior Yoga Psychology Global Online 300 Yoga Alliance School, fusing yoga, psychology, meditation, breathwork, prayer, mindfulness, neuroscience, mindfulness, spirituality, stress + emotional resilience, personal development, leadership, shadow and soul work, somatic mind-body-soul trauma release methods. We offer a Done for You (DFY) system program and more. Explore at IG handle @wisemindsoulwarrioryoga .

Our program supports yoga teachers, wellness entrepreneurs, businesswomen, mompreneurs, and all level students whether they choose to teach yoga, breath-work, meditation, mindfulness, yoga psychology, or not.

It is my life's work, purpose, and passion to guide students to heal intergenerational trauma through somatic yoga psychology work. I am inspired to teach yoga psychology techniques of self-awareness that lead to holistic transformation.

Daring to Be Small...
Daring to Be Seen

After being on the conception journey for far too long, I recognized something vital — here I was trying to conceive a baby but feeling utterly disconnected from my own body. The struggle to succeed was weighing down upon me so badly that I did not realize my body was nowhere on the same page. It was as if the success of this journey defined my true worth.

Truth was, I did not know who I was, did not have a sense of self, and I needed these struggles and stories to define me. To realize how grossly inadequate I felt in my own self was appalling to me.

As I reflected more, it dawned on me that my life until then was actually a mere reflection of what others thought about me. If they approved, I was good; if there were parts of me they disapproved of, then I fervently tried to change them to suit their opinions. Doing so all my life, I felt like a chameleon; I could fit myself anywhere, change to what others liked, and I wouldn't be rejected. I recalled a childhood memory that had stopped me in my tracks.

As a young girl, I was very expressive and active. Not the chubby poster child but a wild spirit indeed. Growing up during times when smartphones and the internet did not exist, playtime outside was my favorite part of the day.

We played this game where we would step-walk in a rhythm and, in the end, click our hips sideways with the girl beside us. It was a lot of fun, and we often found ourselves giggling because at least one of us skipped the beat and had no one to click hips with. One time, my close friend abruptly declared that she did not want me by her side because I was too bony, and it poked her when we hit our hips. The rest of the girls followed suit, and I stood there confused and ashamed. The incident shook me.

Until then, it had never occurred to me that my body size or how bony or chubby my hips were ever mattered in a game, but sadly, this was only the beginning of what would become a long-term relationship being reduced to a body proportion that was determined by a stereotypical construct.

Unknown to me at the time, I was being fed lessons (mostly BS) in the perception of beauty and "good enough" being that perfect body size, skin color, privileges, background, etc., which I was gulping down and believing. The messaging became very clear to me as I grew up — being skinny and short was inadequate, and I could not be considered beautiful or enough whatsoever. Instead of feeling at home in my own skin, my body became an inconvenience.

As a kid, I did not know that I was a sensitive empath; I could easily sense into what others felt, even when unsaid. At times, close relatives would call me out in social gatherings to comment and advise me to overcome my thinness (which was a perceived weakness). It seemed as though the shaming of a thinner individual fell through the cracks and people assumed that it would be taken as a compliment and nothing hurtful.

Fact: Body Shaming is hurtful, whether thin or fat.

Added to what I already felt, I was taking on the weight of others' judgments which seemed to drive home the point of "not good enough" even faster and stronger. The inadequacy kept marinating inside, and I was steadily disconnecting from my body, became disembodied, and lived more in my head. I could hardly feel the chair I sat on or my feet touching the ground.

My self-confidence took a hit, and I continually juggled thoughts of how I looked. Was this dress fitting me, or would I be ridiculed? Will I be seen, and appreciated, invited to that cool party? Will I be included in the dances and the school plays? I was often overwhelmed around people, jaw clenched, hypervigilant, and bracing for an impending insult. My posture changed, and I started to shrink, appearing even smaller than I seemed. I felt diminished and unimportant. Trapped in my own small confines of safety, it felt better being invisible. Self-preservation became my sole goal.

Feeling unworthy of love and belonging, I took to other ways of finding comfort — People-pleasing was one of them. I began to overextend and became that wise, insightful friend whom anyone could lean on for emotional and other support. I relished the idea because it made me feel needed but left me overwhelmed and depleted. I kept choosing roles that did not put me in the spotlight while I toiled very hard in the background. No number of academic accolades compensated for the inadequacy I felt within. I kept trying to measure my worthiness using someone else's yardstick.

This internalized shame of being lesser than and not good enough was the underbelly of my relationships, including my marriage. My desire to become a mother took longer than I imagined, and during this time, all my earlier fears and emotions that I had so neatly locked away now re-surfaced and nearly broke my marriage. The shame and wounding had festered far too long, and it was time for some brave action.

This was a crisis and my wake-up call that I couldn't ignore any longer. I had to find a way to reconnect with my body and make it my own if I was to get out of this helpless victim loop.

This became a pivotal point in my life; honoring my body and reclaiming the power back became a journey that changed everything for me.

"When I discover who I am, I'll be free."
— Ralph Ellison

I enrolled in belly dance, something I had secretly hoped to learn when I was younger but was too scared to face ridicule. The initial days of joining the class were the most torturous ones. I had to look at my small body in a studio full of mirrors. Every direction reflected the smallness of me and, with it all, the trauma that I had associated with. But the support I received from my teacher and companions at the studio was priceless. Instead of judging, they welcomed the diversity of our bodies — big, small, large, thin, it did not matter. For perhaps the first time in my adult life, I realized I could access that wild-spirited inner child inside of me. She took to dancing like a body parched for fluidity and nourishment.

It surprised me that I could dance and enjoy the connection again. I felt a sense of aliveness flowing through my veins and a fierceness that followed after. I kept to a journaling practice and explored the old stories that came up often. It helped me trace my behavior patterns to childhood or other earlier versions of myself.

Little by little, I allowed myself kindness (which I gave to others in loads) to be directed to my own body. As I expressed and at times reached out for support, it was a cathartic process to witness the trauma, heal it and call these vital soul pieces back home.

The more I healed from this inherent, deep-rooted sense of shame, the more I was looking at how far spread this pattern was. Feeling "not ever quite enough" was like a cellular imprint that was passed on across generations, lineages, and societies, and I began to see it in varying degrees in most women I met. I was touching the edges of a wounding that patriarchy had set us all up with.

I realized that when I was younger, I did not quite know that I could oppose the views of others who commented on or ridiculed me. The reason is that the culture I grew up in already had pre-standards and stereotyped versions of being beautiful, powerful, etc. If it wasn't people, then films and ads did the rest to perpetuate these perfectly endowed versions of women. Confusing times! In contrast to providing a safe space where I could feel accepted and nurtured, societies and communities — due to these conditioned cultural beliefs and stories — were, in fact, becoming toxic environments where it was difficult to grow and flourish.

Being far away from home helped me reach out for support that was not going to re-traumatize me but become my source of comfort during intense times. I found support in communities and companions who had similar experiences where I did not have to conform to outdated ideologies.

I invested in therapy to go deeper with the underlying layers that felt tricky to shift or too intense to move through without a trusted witness who could help me find my light again.

For the longest time, what I truly desired was colored by how much I deserved or what was allowed by other people, including authority figures in life. The programming I received from my schooling and upbringing strengthened the perception even more.

It wasn't easy, but this crisis in identity and self-worth was connecting me to deeper parts of myself, that which I had rejected earlier and wished to never look at. The fear of consequences, of breaking the rules if I followed my heart, was a hard one to flip. It was hard not to fall back on the old patterns of putting others first, but my commitment to change was greater. The uncoupling of my self-worth to others' opinions was one hard lesson to crack. But I slowly learned how to see myself and the many gifts that were lying inside hidden all along. I realized I was a creative person, something I'd never considered myself before! I committed to drawing healthy boundaries and saying "no" when I had to without guilt.

Journaling helped me become aware of my core patterns and what I was reflecting out into the world. I realized that being an empath, I was absorbing the feelings of others around me, and criticism was bogging me down quite deeply. So, I resorted to people-pleasing to keep them happy as well as protect myself from any painful comments about my body. But now, I could flip it and use my empathic abilities as a gift to understand myself better as well as connect to others in a more empowered manner.

The longer I gave myself permission to listen and communicate with my body, the greater the strength I could draw from within. We became allies, and I finally found peace within my own skin.

I saw that I was bringing so much into the world just by being me. In fact, I was enough!

This became an initiation into a path of integrity and radical self-acceptance toward my body. It not only was a journey of unwinding and healing for me but also fueled my passion to truly extend my support to other women who were struggling with these limiting beliefs, especially of the culture they were born into sabotaging their lives and authentic expression.

The layers keep coming off, and the transformation continues, but to live the embodiment I truly desire is an ongoing endeavor.

What I thought was a pit stop on my fertility road transformed me from being a doormat to opening the door to my own empowerment and that of others. Growth and transformation of an individual can seldom be singular; the nature of it is to ripple out and touch others to create more ripples. The nudge to support others to find their way back to the light within themselves, that hardly had anything to do with the outside stories and beliefs became my mission.

I realized my empathic abilities were, in fact, a gift to understand others and help them navigate tough spots with more ease and support, which became the foundation of my services as a trusted companion and an intuitive coach.

Looking back, I realize now that my life was not just a shade of gray; it was, in fact, a colorful tapestry of experiences. My body temple is exquisite in all its variations and does not have to conform to anything to be perfect.

Healing, transforming, and receiving those beautiful parts of me that were too scared to walk home or recoiled at ridicule may not be a task done in a single day, but the process has brought me to the truth that no matter what, my soul never stopped shining her light. All I had to do was keep the door open.

About Aparna Vemula

Aparna Vemula is a contributing author to the "*Soul Shine Collaborative 2022.*" Born and raised in India, she currently resides in the USA with her husband.

The world of words has been her constant companion in life, and this is her first time dipping her toes into becoming an author. Drawing from her early experiences, growing up in spaces of inhibition, the core of her story is about turning around the inadequacy often perceived around body image as a catalyst to actually embracing the imperfect perfection lying deep within. She loves to bring this work to others, to share the light that has kindled within, and watch others come alive too.

She is the owner of whisper within and an intuitive coach who loves to support women in letting go of old, disempowering stories that have mired them down for years — perhaps even decades, to feeling lighter, freer, and experiencing more joy, vitality, and playfulness in their life.

https://whisperwithin.me/

Reclaiming Wild Creativity

An Initiation

Dusk is falling; inside the yurt, the light is dim. Candles cast flickering shadows in the circle of space between me and my guide, and I'm warmed, from my right, by the wood-burning stove. I smell sage and the musty scents of autumn arriving in the woodland. The tinkling babble of the stream outside echoes the excitement in my belly as my closing ceremony commences.

I'm on retreat on rewilded land in west Wales at the home of my friend and guide, Brier. Three quiet and private days have reenergized me as I've marveled at butterflies, stared into the pond, rocked in the hammock, journeyed with the drum, and walked in the woods.

Towards the end of my ceremony, I'm invited to read a piece I've written about the being I met a couple of weeks back and who has revealed her name to me today.

As I finish, I long to claim and keep her, but this is, I intuitively know, an initiation. Despite my fear that she'll cease to be — that she'll leave me — and that this is all a flight of my imagination, I take the pages and offer them one by one to the flames.

As the words burn, she doesn't leave but, instead, solidifies within and comes to rest — curled like a fox in a den — deep within my belly. My womb.

It is only then that I truly understand.

It was never a question of claiming her. *She* is guiding *me* home.

Lost in the Forest

Two decades ago — when I was in my early thirties — I experienced burnout in my corporate career and a clinical depression that took over twelve months to recover from. I've been reeling and healing from the wounds of that time ever since.

Having regained the strength and confidence to re-establish my career for a few more years, by the time I was 40, I finally knew I was done. I had to find a different path. I needed more freedom, and I wanted to explore my neglected and relatively untapped creativity.

By 2009, my husband and I had left our jobs, relocated, gone mortgage-free, and each established part-time businesses. We shared a commitment to living on a much-reduced income in a simpler, slower, and less materialistic lifestyle.

I thought I'd healed — that I'd found my shine then — but, in truth, I hadn't come close. What I couldn't see — for the decade between 2009 and 2019 and despite a second depression in 2014 — was that whilst the practicalities of my lifestyle had altered for the better, I'd brought outdated and harmful beliefs, assumptions, and needs with me.

I was being creative, yes, and it was — is — my soul's work, but I was living and creating not from my soul but from my ego.

An Epiphany

In the summer of 2019 — after exhibiting for six weeks in a pop-up shop for local artists and creatives that had led to my most lucrative period of sales since I'd first established my business — my epiphany moment came.

I remember how warm the sun was on my upturned face as I watched swifts wheeling around the city sky when the words came: "Stop! This isn't soulful creativity."

I floundered and made no new art as I tried to work out what "soulful creativity" meant. That autumn, I transferred my energy into writing a book that culminated in going on retreat with The Unbound Press in February 2020. There, it became clear to me that replacing one form of creativity for another, pushing and striving for a solution, wasn't the answer. I gave up writing too.

The connections I made through those few months of Unbound writing have been part of the arc of my story.

They've led to this piece, to new ideas about unbinding, and to my connection with Brier.

Sometimes what we think we are looking for when we take one path isn't what the Universe intended for us at all.

I Reclaim My Soul Skin

Soon after the writing retreat — just one month or so — the U.K. went into its first lockdown.

As an introvert, I benefited enormously from the enforced break in social demands, but I still wanted creative connection, and so, in April 2020, I joined an online circle called "Fairy Tale Medicine."

Over the course of a year, we spent two months at a time immersing in each of six "fairy" stories, meeting in circle weekly to share discoveries and truths. At the heart of all the stories and the experiences we shared was the examination and healing of the conditioning that denies us our "wildness."

The final tale of the six was that of the Selkie — a shapeshifting seal who becomes trapped on land in human form and bribed into marriage and motherhood by the man who has stolen her skin from the shoreline and hidden it from her.

It's a powerful story about choices, lost connections, and reclamation, and as we explored it — and my hands chose to create seals from clay — I found myself musing on and reclaiming aspects of myself that had been neglected, wounded, and buried since childhood. Things like my love of spontaneity, purposeless play, encounters in nature, open-minded wonder and curiosity, exploration, imagination, and make-believe. Medicine indeed.

I saw how, in my late teens and twenties, I'd become attached to proving my worth and justifying my life choices through education and a career. I'd broken the mold of the female in my family by going to university and choosing work over having children and always felt a little like a misfit because of it. When I chose to give up that path — but still clear that I didn't want a family — I simply transferred this need to prove something onto my creativity.

Creativity in that form was about proving something outside of myself as measured by others rather than about authentically exploring and expressing what was at the heart of me. While it was externally focused and motivated, it was never going to be, or feel, soulful.

As we explored the wild feminine within the stories, I learned how living this way had buried some of my deepest values and my innate feminine qualities. I'd become overly reliant on masculine qualities like competitiveness, logical thinking, reason, direct action, and analysis, which were highly rewarded in the environment in which I worked. This came at the expense of potent aspects of my creative feminine energy, some of which had been shamed and repressed; qualities like depth, receptivity, sensitivity, intuition, and flow lay dormant and neglected within.

I'd brought so much old, outdated and conditioned "stuff" into the new lifestyle we'd envisioned. No wonder things hadn't felt soulful or led to the deep-rooted sense of meaning, fulfillment, and contentment I sought.

It was time to reclaim my soul skin and return to my natural habitat.

She Who Welcomed Me Home

So, who was it who guided me home at that ceremony in the yurt in September 2021, just a few months after I'd swum with the Selkies?

Her name is TenderWild, and she is my "wild creative" essence: the source of my soul shine.

Rewilding My Creativity

In the past twelve months or so, through healing my deepest wounds through fairy tale medicine and meeting TenderWild, I've felt soulfulness infusing my creative expression.

At the heart of this has been a process of rewilding in which

- I'm operating from an entirely new set of values, inspirations, and motivations and have disentangled from making art as a product and seeing my creativity in commercial terms. I've tentatively returned to selling but only decide that *after* a piece has emerged.

- I take extended breaks from social media when I need to so that I can listen for my authentic inner inspirations and yearnings. Ideas — that carry my own unique essence — land beautifully without the endless distraction and comparison.

- I'm awakening a sense of spirituality and reciprocity through mindful and conscious connection with nature on the land around me.

- I'm making art that comes from my soul even when it's not great technically and with no idea if anyone else will understand it, respond to it, or like it. I feel like I should whisper this, but my inner critic and perfectionist have all but disappeared!

- I'm communicating monthly with a growing community through an email I send called "Wild Creative Musings." I love sharing my experiences and receiving replies from other rewilders and soulful creatives.

- I'm focusing on eight essential feminine qualities that I have rediscovered at my core, and I'm learning how to celebrate them. There may even be a book to be written about them one day!

- I'm making peace with what the pandemic taught me about the deepest needs of my introverted nature, and

I've created clearer boundaries around my preference for space, peace, quiet, and privacy.

- I'm allowing my creativity to be spontaneous and unplanned. I set very few goals or targets and rarely make plans.

- I flow with the energy of pieces I'm working on and always have several projects on the go at any one time (when I recently discovered a 2015 TEDTalk by Emilie Wapnick about the multi-potentialite, it REALLY landed for me!)

- I work with seasons and cycles and no longer need to be active and productive all the time.

- I'm learning that each creative impulse, idea, and piece has its own energy. I'm simply a conduit for creativity to emerge. I love giving myself over to that; it makes the process of creating feel alchemical.

Wild Creativity is Soulful Creativity

As a result of rewilding my creativity, my focus has changed, my priorities have shifted, and my needs and values have become sentinels.

I can be nothing other than soulful when I anchor into this free, expressive, curious, playful, unself-conscious, experimental, sensitive, loving, and creative self.

Connected to "TenderWild" inside, I can do nothing other than shine with the light of the wild and soulful creative energy burning within.

About Alison Roe

Alison Roe is an artist and creative based in Herefordshire, U.K.. She lives slowly and simply and connects regularly to her love of nature, folklore and traces of the ancient past.

Aged forty, Ali escaped the corporate treadmill to recover from the burnout and depression it had caused. A decade-long journey of healing has followed — with many U-turns and bumps in the road — that's helped her to access the soulfulness that swirls within, understand her core needs, and reclaim a sense of authentic creative expression.

Now — with her soul reconnected to, and anchored in, its tender wildness — Ali feels that she is living her truest and deepest sense of purpose.

To connect with Ali, find her on Instagram @aliroecreative, where there's also a link to her website and free monthly publication, "This Tender Wildness."

The Alchemy of a Soulmate Relationship

My heart broke open. I sat at my computer typing and typing from the heart to this creative guy I was infatuated with. Then, with my heart still wide open, I got that beautiful taste of spiritual love where everything is brighter, and you feel connected to everything. But it became a prelude to my creativity going out of control. As the creative part of me burst into awareness, breaking me out of my rigidly academic thinking, it led me into the darkest depths of my mind, leaving a traumatic wound locked up inside. But in locking it up, I built a solid wall around my heart that kept all romance and notions of creativity firmly at a distance.

Over a decade later, that locked-up wound began to make itself known. Here I was with a guy I'd worked hard to manifest. I'd done all the law of attraction things — visualized what I wanted, cleared out old patterns, and taken action. My chosen form of action was speed dating. We had an instant connection, and the four-minute speed date was more than enough time to know there was mutual attraction. All that manifesting stuff was working.

But my anxieties gradually got exposed. An anxiety attack came out of nowhere while driving from a family party to see him. As we dated more, I started fading away — molding and squashing myself into who I thought would be the perfect girlfriend for him. But I was trying so hard to please without any real communication about what would actually make either of us happy.

He dumped me right around the six-week mark. I'd never had a relationship go past that six-week mark and I'd always been the one to run first. It devastated my ego dreams to be dumped and to not make it past that six-week milestone.

What was wrong with me?

Why was I so hopeless?

I'd worked so hard to clear all of my beliefs, so why wasn't it working?

I managed to bury the anxiety but out of the blue, a deep, cold terror chilled my mind and body. I tried all of the tools I had — energy healing, journaling, ThetaHealing — and none of them could reach this terror. Realizing it was beyond what I could cope with on my own, I reasoned that I needed to find the origin of the problem in a past life with this guy. I'd simply go back to the past life with him in hypnosis, fix the problems we had, and then he'd come back to me.

I contacted a hypnotherapist whom I knew did past-life regression, and the next day, I drove 45 minutes to her house for a session. Sitting on her sofa, tears poured down as I sobbed and explained my problems. She told me that these weren't issues that could be resolved in one session. I'd need a course of sessions.

With tears still pouring down my cheeks, I sat in her comfy therapy armchair, reclining back as she played soothing music and gently took me into a peaceful trance. By the end of the session, the tears were gone, and I felt 100 times better.

I was excited to try out more hypnotherapy and would look forward to each session. It was an inner adventure of imagination. I saw myself as a queen in one life and as someone rescuing my trapped father in another life. There were times when I'd go so deep into a trance that I wouldn't remember anything but would feel the deep rest I'd received. And other times, I'd feel all kinds of energy moving through me while my hypnotherapist noticed colored energies around me. Some spiritual consciousness was helping me heal.

In the meantime, I was feeling much calmer about the breakup and started online dating. Initially saying "yes" to any guy who wanted to chat or ask me out, I soon learned to set more boundaries. To check their profile for a fit and remember the dating pool is an ocean of insecurity — and to not take that personally. My hypnotherapist encouraged me to write a list of everything I wanted in a partner, and I used my online profile like a vision board calling out to the one for me.

After my course of hypnotherapy was over, I got the opportunity to help out at a flirting workshop. The workshop leader held the most beautiful, safe space while we explored her activities. First, we got into a playful mood, thinking about what activities brought out our fun, flirty side — for me, it was the roller-disco. Then we did an activity that had a profound effect on me. We had to gaze into the eyes of a partner and takes turns to give and receive the gaze. It felt unnervingly vulnerable to receive, and I immediately saw an unhealed pattern in myself. It was so much easier to give — it gave a sense of control but receiving? That felt overpowering. The realization set off a chain reaction in my psyche, wrapping up the work from the hypnotherapy. The hypnotherapy had worked on the level of the mind, and this was working at the level of emotion and body. I sobbed loudly in the car on the way home as I felt chunks of stagnant, blocked energy breaking free from my solar plexus and sacral centers.

Two weeks later, I joined a dating website called "Yoga Singles" and soon received a message from a guy who looked pretty interesting but lived over a hundred miles away. Our message exchange lasted all of two messages and died off.

In the meantime, I went speed dating again and met a lovely local journalist. Around the same time, I trained as a ThetaHealing instructor — a modality oriented towards opening to the love of the "creator-of-all-that-is." It was a fabulous week of energy healing and psychic explorations, but this journalist couldn't understand what I was talking about. I realized I needed someone I could talk with about energy and healing, but with so few men at this kind of training, I doubted I'd find anyone.

A few weeks later, I got another message on Yoga Singles from the guy who lived too far away. But this time, he'd got a job at an eco-center in the county I was in and was moving closer to me. He invited me to meet up and see how things went. I told him that the only eco-center I knew was The Sustainability Centre. I knew it because that was where my dad was buried — the most incredible natural burial — shortly after I plunged into the darkest depths of my mind. That's where this guy's new job was. I'd just moved closer to the eco-center too. Could these be signs? I didn't dare hope.

Before our first date, I went to visit the tree we planted on Dad's grave and pondered all that had happened since the tumultuous year Dad died. Then I made my way to the pub to meet the guy. As soon as he walked in and our eyes met, I knew there was something special between us.

His name was Tony. He made me laugh a lot, and we talked for hours about travel, art, ancestors, and spirituality. The date ended with a romantic kiss under a clear starry sky. This time there was no feeling of rush or a need to force it to last. It felt more natural.

I nervously waited for the crucial six-week milestone, and this time, I made it. The connection was strong, and he ticked off 90% of the list of things I wanted in a partner. It was looking like I'd finally, finally done it. After 20 years of failing at romantic relationships, this one was lasting.

He was working as an accommodation manager, but really, he was an artist — another creative. It was like life knew I'd get too scared if he came into my life as a creative, so I needed him in disguise as a manager to feel safe. For the first couple of years, he was too busy with his full-time jobs to make much art — and perhaps my deep fears were blocking him too.

This powerful love connection began its alchemy — drawing out impurities to help us come into purer connection with that universal spiritual force in all things. Our inner-child insecurities and protective strategies came up. A few times it seemed like we would break up, but each time something would shift, we'd communicate deeper, and our relationship would become stronger.

I trained in hypnotherapy myself and learned to release more relationship patterns. All the while, I joined an expensive business coaching program that had the worst conditions for getting in touch with my own creativity. The creative wound got louder and louder, and I crashed out of the business coaching program, hitting rock bottom. I experienced despair and powerlessness that forced me to change course. I plunged myself into the Unbound writing mastermind.

Far from being creative, my writing went all over the place and just seemed to be rant after rant. But I was getting curious about sacred geometry — the idea of underlying order and structure in nature. Tony, too, was exploring sacred geometry, beginning a project to build 3D sacred geometry shapes out of wood. Gradually, my writing led me deeper and deeper inside myself. Each rant creating a sense of safety inside as I wrote deeper truths instead of hiding behind false masks. Eventually, it was safe enough to touch the wound inside, to heal it and let go of the powerful protection around it.

I made the decision to join a collaborative book to get experience with sharing my story and publishing. I'd been exploring story writing structures in online writing groups, and synchronicity had brought me one writing structure in particular called "Save The Cat," used by Hollywood screenwriters and novelists. Save The Cat set off sparks of excitement and joy inside. It was another example of the deeper structure and order behind creation. Writing my story with it stirred up my whole psyche, and things between Tony and me once again seemed to take us to the edge of finishing. We'd survived six weeks, and now we'd reached six years. Maybe we wouldn't survive.

It all felt so messy and turbulent that I turned to my hypnotherapy teacher and writing coach for support. My hypnotherapy teacher took me into a powerful process of uncovering the wounds of female ancestors and the divine feminine inside, while my writing coach reassured me that the relationship turbulence could simply be an opportunity to connect deeper than ever with Tony. And it was. We survived again and connected deeper.

A month later, my story got published in the collaborative book *INTUITIVE — Speaking Her Truth*. I soon learned that if I'd thought writing the story was powerful, publishing it would be even more powerful. Planning to spend launch day messaging people and sending them the link to buy the e-book, instead, I was confined to the bathroom as a urinary tract infection reached its peak right as the book was coming out in the U.K.. Half impressed at the synchronistic timing of the peak of this problem and half alarmed at what was happening to my body, I thought creativity seemed to be too powerful for me.

Once the paperback version came out and I was holding it in my hands, it felt more real. I felt intuitively guided to connect with the hurting and confused younger version of myself who'd gotten overpowered by creativity all those years ago. I went into a visualization and imagined handing her the book as I explained she'd written a chapter for it. Her eyes widened in disbelief and a smile of delight shone on her face. It was inconceivable to her that she'd ever do anything creative, let alone have any creative success in her own right. She was going to be a good little wifey and support her husband's creative success. In that visualization process, it suddenly became clear — her infatuation with the creative guy all those years ago was really about seeing her own hidden creative potential in him. And it scared her.

The safety and alchemy of a strong, truthful soulmate relationship helped me reach the creative wound and heal it. Writing and publishing my story helped me recover a vital piece of who I really am and helped to heal the wounds of the inner feminine. The inner feminine was finally able to work together with the inner masculine to reach the kind of creativity that flows from a spiritual source. The kind of creativity that lights up your soul to shine.

About Jacqui McGinn

Jacqui is an energy healer, qualified hypnotherapist, writer and teacher of ESOL and Japanese. She is based in the U.K. and works internationally online. Jacqui is perhaps one of the most unique people you'll meet because she speaks fluent Japanese and can play the bagpipes.

Jacqui is fascinated by language, symbols, stories and all the ways humans share or hide deeper truths about themselves. Her love of languages led her to study linguistics at Edinburgh University, and she originally intended to use that love to help people as a speech and language therapist. But she ended up being the perfect candidate for the Japan Exchange and Teaching (JET) program and stayed in Japan for over nine years.

In her first year there, she was devastated by her father's cancer diagnosis and that set off spiritual soul searching. Not long after, she began to experience strange synchronicity with a singer/songwriter and believed he must be "the one." Around the same time, her father's cancer came back. The enormous psychological pressure and confusion ultimately lead to a frightening breakdown, followed by her father's death two weeks later.

Jacqui has come to realize that these events were an invitation from her soul to find out who she really is and share the wisdom of her wound to help others. Jacqui helps her clients get in touch with their own souls for deep healing and guidance and to be able to share the wisdom of their own wounds.

jacquimcginn.com

You Are So Loved

Do you also long to hear the words: You are so loved?

I know I ached to hear these words for many years.

I longed to experience the meaning behind the words, the truth in these words. I was longing for love for most of my life.

You are so loved are words that connect to our soul and make it shine. Our true essence is love.

Unfortunately, we often look for love in the wrong places, till we finally realize we were loved all along and that we were always loved.

My Wakeup Call

Many years ago, I woke up one morning and realized I had no idea who I was any longer. My marriage had just ended, and I had to rebuild my life while being the sole caregiver for my three young kids.

I realized I had been bending over backward to make my marriage work, to make my husband happy. Of course, it didn't work, and I lost myself in the process of it.

That morning, I knew something had to change. I learned to reconnect with myself and went on the journey of recovering from being a doormat.

I had to learn to heal from an emotionally abusive relationship while learning to accept myself just the way I am. I also needed to learn to set up healthy boundaries.

Let me share my story with you, a story of how a child who grew up feeling unloved becomes a people-pleaser and then heals.

Early Years

I grew up feeling like I didn't fit in, that something was definitely wrong with me.

I felt guilty for being the reason my parents had to marry. Without me coming along, I felt they could have been happier with other people. You see, I was an accident, an unplanned child. Of course, as a child, I equated unplanned with unwanted.

Nowadays, I understand that just because your parents didn't plan to have you, you are not necessarily unwanted. Life has a way of giving us the exact things we need to grow.

When I was a child, I never felt loved. All I ever wanted was to be loved. I tried everything to get loving attention, and I learned that when I was the nice girl, my parents liked me. So, I tried hard to be the good girl, the girl my parents could be proud of, the girl who pleased them. Of course, now I understand that my parents had their own stuff to deal with and tried their best, along with their baggage of upbringing.

The People-Pleaser Was Born

I did not speak up. I hid myself. I learned that when I spoke up for myself, I was scolded, that I was not liked, so I tried even harder to be the good girl around my parents.

Being the oldest of three girls, I also fell into the role of being the helper. I had to step up and help my mother out. I could not make my mom's life even harder. She was busy with my younger sisters and had no time or energy for me.

I knew I'd better behave and be a good girl, so my mother would be happy with me.

As children, we are so in tune with our parents that we take on their pain and hurt and try to make them happy. We start mothering them.

The Habit Continued

Being the eternal people-pleaser worked well also in my marriage, where I tried everything to please my ex-husband. Bending over backward till I nearly broke, I was feeling so tired — extremely exhausted on every level — yet I just kept going anyways. That's what good mothers do, right?

We were a family. All I ever wanted was a happy family for my children, never mind the toll it took on me.

Then one day, my marriage ended, and I needed to learn to stand up for myself. I had to keep it all together for my three young children — while re-learning who I was.

I had lost complete sense of who I was, doing everything in my power to make my marriage work, to please my husband, and take care of everyone around me.

Journey to Rediscovering

After my marriage ended, I learned a lot about myself. I realized I am an empath and an introvert, a sensitive soul — everything started to make so much more sense.

I finally felt like I was not alone in the world, that there were others I could relate to, and that nothing was wrong with me. I felt I could finally connect to my soul.

Healing from my emotionally abusive relationship (my husband was a narcissist) truly helped me understand how people-pleasing is not the answer to fill the void of feeling the need to be loved for who we are.

Another Lesson

It took another unhealthy relationship for me to finally realize that I was needy when it came to love — that I only ever felt loved when I was in a relationship.

I felt so lonely, so unloved in this relationship. It reminded me that the time to heal –in big ways — had just begun.

- Time to re-connect with the love within.
- Time to learn to accept myself just the way I am.
- Time to learn to embrace myself fully.

And finally, I was able to say to *myself*, "I love you. You are so loved," from the bottom of my own heart.

What a liberation. My soul was finally shining, and I felt truly connected to the love I was always craving.

Love is Always the Answer

We all come from love, we all go back to love, and here while we are in our human form, we are all looking for love in one form or another.

We might look for the love we crave in others, in food, in alcohol, in games, or in buying or collecting things. Do these other things ever truly make us feel loved?

Maybe for a fleeting moment, we might feel good.

True love only ever comes from within ourselves.

Are you ready to embark on a journey of love, to reconnect with what your soul is asking you for?

I'd love to inspire you with three tips that have helped me along my path:

Ho'oponopono, the Ancient Hawaiian Forgiveness Ritual

Learning to forgive yourself is an essential part of self-love and healing. I love to do the Ho'oponopono ritual in front of a mirror while looking myself in the eye. I repeat the short sentences that make up this ritual out loud seven times (seven is a magical number).

- I apologize/I'm sorry.
- Please forgive me.
- I love you (include your name).
- Thank you.

The beauty of this ritual is that you don't need to know what you forgive yourself for. Just do it; it will feel so liberating. Self-love starts with self-forgiveness.

Hugs

Hug yourself. Yes, hugs are very healing. Wrap your arms around yourself and lean into your hug, breathing in the good feelings.

Now switch your arms — the one that was on top goes underneath now. Yes, this might feel a bit uncomfortable at first.

Tell yourself that you accept all the parts of yourself and that you will learn to love your faults and shadows, too.

Learn to hug the parts of yourself you do not feel so comfortable with yet.

Hugs are amazing, and we, of all people, deserve our own hugs and affection. This exercise is a wonderful way to learn to love your entire being, faults and all.

Give Thanks to Your Body

We all have parts we are critical about. If you'd like to work on acceptance, start to observe your thoughts when you look in the mirror. Where does your inner critic go? Your belly? Your behind? Your thighs?

I was always very critical of my belly. Yes, it was too big, so I loathed that part of me.

Then I learned to be grateful for my belly, the belly that grew three gorgeous children within, the one that expanded and nurtured and nourished my kids. I was amazed at what my belly could do and how it adjusted and helped me become a mother.

If you are critical of your thighs, make sure to think about how they keep you strong and standing, and they help you make the strides necessary to take you wherever you want to go.

Take time to find the good in the perceived "not good enough" parts.

Give thanks to every part of you.

Next time you put your body lotion on, tell each part of your body that you love it.

Our bodies serve us well and give us this gorgeous earthly experience. Let your soul shine by being grateful for your body.

Are You Ready to Let Your Soul Shine?

Keep doing the three practices above, till one day you can stand in front of the mirror, look yourself in the eye, and say ...

You are so loved

to yourself. Let that feeling flow and feel it coming from your heart. You will feel your whole body shine and vibrate with the love you've been longing for. You will feel your mind celebrating — and yes, your soul will be shining brighter than it was before!

You are so worthy of your own love. Never forget that you — of all people — deserve your own love, too.

Sending you so much love,

Caroline

About Caroline Palmy

Caroline Palmy is an award-winning author, speaker, and heart flow healer

who helps gorgeous empaths, sensitive souls, earth angels, and giving hearts to feel good about themselves, helps them lead a life full of joy, find purpose, and finally feel worthy.

She gives you HOPE through her unique process of:

Healing your past

Opening your heart

Prioritizing yourself

Emerge, Evolve and Empower Yourself.

Her first book, *Conversations With Me*, was published in 2018 and won a mention on Janey Loves Platinum Award List.

Her second book, *Loving Conversations With Me*, was published in 2019 and went on the Amazon bestseller list.

Caroline lives in Switzerland with her three young adult children, a golden retriever, a cat, and eight tortoises in a location that allows her to be surrounded by nature.

You can find out more about her and her offers on her website: https://carolinepalmy.com/

A Reconnection to The Feminine and Coming Back Home to Our Soul

When pondering the topic of soul shine, I was called to reflect on the times when I had dimmed my light to fit in. To remember the times when it felt uncomfortable or even dangerous to express being me.

There were times when I felt unsafe to express my creativity, spirituality, and gifts. The times I kept quiet, silent, and favored fitting in over being my weird self. Taking people-pleasing to award-winning extremes, where I shrunk myself or completely hid away in fear. And let me tell you, there were a lot of examples!

Being too quiet, too loud, too friendly, too honest, too outspoken, too flirty, too sexual, too thin, too ridiculous, too weird, too deep, too emotional, too intimidating, and even having too much personality.

As we continue to journey through the hangover of patriarchy, whatever we wear, do or say, we are judged and rated. Many women end up hiding their light and people-pleasing because they don't feel safe in the world. Trying to be quieter or smaller and not take up too much space. As a society, we have become disconnected from the feminine energy, within and without.

Disconnected from the earth.

Disconnected from our intuition and flow.

Encouraged to hustle and go with the grind.

Disconnected from our innate, cyclical nature.

Disconnected from each other.

Disconnected from our bodies.

Our energy.

Our heart.

Our soul.

Something that struck me was that many of the most significant and traumatic experiences that have held me back from being me, at least in this lifetime, had stemmed from other women. Their bitchiness, judgment, and betrayal understandably led to a deep mistrust of girls and women. Some even admitted they were jealous of me, and at times, I experienced violence. This was the sister wound in all its glory.

I would repeat these stories of rejection to myself, over and over, in a loop of sadness and grief. I hated the thought of others being jealous or not liking me, and this subconsciously led to people-pleasing, staying small, and trying to fit in. I realize now, this was a trauma response to protect and take care of myself. I have no shame in doing these things. But in doing so, trying to hold back was also painful and self-abandoning.

There came a point where I had to look at those patterns and see my role and how I was allowing myself to be treated. These were not the kind of people I wanted to have in my life, and I realized I deserved better and had to let people go. It was challenging and took courage to get out of those situations and relationships. Another part of this was recovering from co-dependency. Putting others first whilst disregarding my own needs was exhausting and often not as healthy or helpful to others as I thought. It was also a clever distraction, drawing my attention away from my own pain. Making these changes wasn't easy, and as someone who didn't like to rock the boat, at times, it felt excruciating. But it got easier with practice. These painful experiences forced me to create strong, loving boundaries. I no longer tolerate bitchiness in friendships or people who are abusive. Now I have amazing friendships and much healthier relationships.

The wound of the witch lives within many women. Whether they consider themselves a witch or not, there is a huge fear holding women back from expressing them-selves and sharing their voices. When women do identify as being a witch — or labels that link to this, such as a healer — there is a collective resistance, resulting in hiding their magic and true nature. This can be related to their current life experience and also runs deeply into ancestral and past-life threads. This affects all genders in obvious and subtle ways we often aren't aware of, but I notice prevalence particularly in women I work with and have journeyed through this personally.

Within my journey of healing and reclaiming the feminine, the wound of the witch has been a big part of that journey. In a past life, I was a white witch and helped others through herbal medicine and energy healing. I was betrayed by people I loved and then killed. I became aware of this trauma around eight years ago. I noticed how it was affecting me and felt terrified to share about my current work and felt a real fear of being killed for doing similar work in this past life.

I had resistance to getting support with this but did eventually (years later). I now help others with past-life work through the Akashic Records and see this pattern a lot.

As well as the trauma, there have been gifts and wisdom I have connected with from this past life as a witch. I even learned that I use similar rituals and work with incense in the same way as I used to, even using the same symbols. I followed my intuition, and it led me back to this inner wisdom. I even got advice from this part of my soul to use mugwort and specific herbs and have always felt a deep resonance to working with plants. When I was younger, I made rose water and perfume from a neighbor's rose garden. Our soul remembers and guides us to things we used to do.

Working with the Akashic Records has taught me a lot about the journey of the soul and gives me the honor of connecting others to their soul. The Akashic Records hold a record of all that has been and the potential future of our soul's journey. This includes this life, past lives, and connections through our ancestral lineage. When we realize how multifaceted our soul is and reconnect with those parts of ourselves we have forgotten, it can be so profound. We are so much more than just our human selves or inner child. Of course, they need to be acknowledged and cared for. But we need to ensure they are not running the show and making our decisions.

It's important to acknowledge the role of privilege, which I continue to learn from. As well as being a woman in this world, being black or a person of color, LGBTQ+, or disabled can make being in this world even more dangerous or challenging. It is important to acknowledge the role that privilege plays. For example, the ways the indigenous tribes have suffered and continue to be exploited. We need to take care and educate ourselves to move through this world with more care for others.

I spoke earlier of disconnection to the feminine and I will share a little about my journey of reconnection.

Reconnecting with the earth has been a key part of my journey spiritually and in healing and reclaiming the feminine. She is the mother. Connecting physically and on an energetic level is so important when doing energy work. The earth and nature around us is a mirror to our inner beauty and wisdom. She tethers us. Particularly for highly sensitive people, we need grounding, and working with the earth is paramount, particularly if our work or play is in other realms. She feeds us and nourishes us in multiple ways. Let's bow to her in awe and deep gratitude and give back. This is a symbiotic relationship.

Coming back to our bodies is also deeply important. It can be easy for magical types to have their head in the stars. We can't truly connect to our intuition or source, without connecting fully to our bodies.

When we believe our worth comes from other people's validation, we will always feel empty. Realizing that not everyone will like you — just as you don't like everyone — is a big step. I mean, some people don't like dogs, and dogs are the best!

I have certainly found that as I get older, I naturally care less about what others think of me. But finding our community is so important. The people who love you in all of your weirdness, who you can be completely yourself with, who nourish your nervous system — these are your people! You don't need to hide or dim. Because they love you as you are. If you don't already have your people, I recommend being more *you*. I have found the more *me* I am, the more wonderful weirdo's find me.

Women's circles have been such medicine for me. I began by attending others' circles and now run my own. This space to be seen, heard, and held is deeply nourishing and reconnects us together in sisterhood, in love and trust, healing through timelines. By coming together and reminding each other, we begin to journey back home to ourselves. Softening deeper into love along the way. We are here to remind each other and guide each other back home to love.

When we walk the path of the healer, this acts as a huge mirror for our own stuff. I believe it's important to honor our humanness. After all, we are souls with human bodies and complicated brains. But we can get so caught up in the humanness that we forget to connect with our souls.

It is time to reconnect with our truth and to express that freely. We are awakening as a collective, healing our traumas, challenges, and fears. We have stayed quiet, conforming, and palatable for too long. It is time to reconnect with our truth and to express that freely. When we come together, we are a force to be reckoned with. We are not alone in this path. We are here to reclaim the lost parts, to heal the challenges, and to remember our true power. As each woman does so, she shows the way to others. Let's be weird and wonderful. These are powerful times we are living in. We are reawakening our voice and reclaiming our power. It is safe now.

About Charley Alcock

I am Charley Alcock, healer, creative, soul guide.

A lover of dogs, sunsets, and dancing in the kitchen. I'm a Yorkshire lass and followed my heart to Bournemouth to live out my mermaid dreams by the sea.

I've journeyed through many challenges and have been on a wild ride of recovery and reclamation. Much of my journey and work is about supporting women to reconnect with their inner peace, power, and wisdom and is often imbued with the path of the feminine and returning to love.

I run women's circles, writing circles, and workshops and work 1:1 in person and online. I offer Akashic readings and healing, where we work through soul embodiment, past lives, and ancestral healing. I run sacred mentorship journeys, Reiki healing and teaching, and bespoke therapy. I have been doing this work for 13 years and love it so much.

If you want to connect, you can find me over on Instagram https://www.instagram.com/charleyalcock. I would love to see you there.

What Would I Do if I Allowed Myself to Dance in the Spotlight?

If you'd asked me five years ago to get in front of a camera in a swimsuit for a picture that would be shared far and wide, the shy side of my nature would have set off numerous red flags, my inner critics screaming about what a bad idea it would be, and my brain would have gone into intricate detail of every possible catastrophic worst-case scenario.

Then I would've done one of a number of things. I might have reluctantly said, "Ok," trying to people-please, not wanting to disappoint or look unwilling, and then built up so much anxiety about it until the time came around. At that point, I would've found an excuse of a terrible lurgy or fictitious injury on the day and left them in the lurch at the last minute, not able to go through with it (which I had probably known since I was asked but never wanted to admit to myself). Then would come the guilt and shame of letting them down which I would use as a stick to beat myself up. I may even have talked myself into actually being unwell because I was fretting about saying "yes" when I meant to say "no." I would also be lambasting myself for not standing my ground, not speaking up and honoring my true feelings when I knew in the moment of being asked that I couldn't actually go through with it, and now I was failing other people.

"If only I had more courage to say what I mean."

"If only I could say the word 'no' when my whole body was screaming it on the inside."

"If only they could have picked up on my unwillingness and let me off the hook without me having to say it."

Or, I may have said "yes" and then spent the intervening period starving myself and shaving every possible strand of body hair, self-tanning to give the impression of looking less bulky, trying on every swimsuit in my drawer to see which gave me the illusion of being slightly smaller, maybe even buying a new one which promised some "tummy control" or "sculpting magic." I'd be practicing poses where I could suck my stomach in, doing that bent knee thing to make my legs look less chunky, remembering not to press my bicep against my side as this spreads the fat and makes the arm look even bigger and flabbier than it is, reminding myself to lower my jaw, but not too much that it exaggerates the double/triple chins.

Then if I actually made it to the shoot after all that, I would have felt incredibly uncomfortable, assuming any passersby were staring and wondering what this fat, pale, wobbly girl in a swimsuit was doing exposing herself on the beach like that. And wondering if the photographer had chosen me to tick a diversity box so they had a range of body shapes — mine being at the larger end of the scale.

Or maybe, just maybe, I would have found the strength to say "no" in the first place, mumbled some excuse, and scuttled away reprimanding myself for being such a coward to miss an experience like that. I did this often for many years, saying "no" to opportunities that would have stretched my comfort zone and ultimately brought me so much joy, but put me far too significantly in the spotlight, too much attention on me.

I would happily jump out of a plane and go backpacking alone but shove a microphone in my hand or ask me an unexpected question in a meeting, and I would freeze and forget every word I'd ever had in my head. The fear of looking like a fool was overwhelming and made me terrified of being around people at times. I wanted to be invited, included, and to join it, but the analysis and overthinking of everything I had said and done in each interaction would utterly exhaust me, as I have realized since I got to know, befriend, and embrace my introversion and anxiety.

If I had gone through with the photoshoot, when I saw the pictures (if the photographer could even get any decent ones with all that going on), I would have zoomed in, looked at the wobbly bits, examined the cellulite, and seen where I didn't suck my stomach in adequately (i.e., enough to make my large, round belly look as flat as an ironing board). I would've then spotted things I hadn't even noticed previously, like the stretch marks on parts of my body I'd not looked at for a while or the red veins that I hadn't seen before.

However, things can change. A few months earlier, I went to have some photos taken by a professional photographer for a swimsuit brand I am a huge fan of. I have been photographed by Justine before, and she captured some incredible images that made me see myself differently. I saw the strength and power within me as I looked at the pictures she'd taken. They appeared in an outdoor swimming magazine, and I had some incredible comments about them. There were some that said I looked beautiful. But that wasn't the point. I think what struck me when I saw the images myself was the potent energy that shone through, the determined look on my face, and the strength and stoicism of this woman who gets into the sea whatever the temperature, all year round. What meant the most to me was when I was told I had inspired other women by being unapologetically me in those pictures and that I was thanked for allowing an un-photoshopped, unfiltered, unaltered body to be seen instead of the usual images we see in swimsuit advertising of a narrow range of small sized bodies, with nicely consistent skin color and tone, and curves in the "right places."

So, with these thoughts as my armor, along with more of the same incredible swimwear as before and some bright lipstick, I headed to the beach. We were blessed with a dazzling sunny and mild January morning and calm waters, and I knew I could get into the sea at some point which was a blessing after a week of high winds and huge waves scuppering my swimming plans. I stood awaiting instructions, feeling confident and comfortable. If I'm not secure on the beach in a swimsuit now, after four years of sea swimming and changing on the seashore in all weathers, I'll never be.

But this was different. Especially when we wandered along to the prom looking for the next spot for some images, surrounded by walkers enjoying the unseasonal balmy sunny weather. I was enjoying seeing people watching me and wondering what was going on. Whenever I see a professional photo shoot on the seafront I wonder if it's someone famous. I didn't imagine once that they might be wondering why someone of my body shape was standing confidently in front of the camera. I just enjoyed their smiles, words of encouragement, and sense of admiration: maybe it was for being in just a swimsuit in January or being in swimwear in public, but either way, I took the gazes as approval.

A little girl passed by pushing her doll in her buggy, and she said to her parents, "Why is that lady having her photo taken?" and I chipped in, "Why not?" And why not, indeed? I hope I have made a tiny contribution to that little girl's perception that all bodies are allowed to be in swimsuits being photographed on the promenade. People of my shape and size have been excluded by the mainstream media for so long. And one of the comments that warms my heart the most from people who follow my social media accounts is, "Thank you for showing us what real bodies look like." And that's just it, isn't it? We are fed such curated, filtered, altered, straight-sized images of women that although we know consciously, we can't and don't all look like that, we can't help our subconscious taking on the message that we should try and look that way. And then add the dysmorphia that can occur so that even if we do look "like that," we don't believe that we do. If all I offer to people is what a real body looks like and the fact that it's possible for anyone to be comfortable in their body without it meeting society's standards of perfection, then I have achieved my goal.

So, whether it is literally dancing in the spotlight or posing in an alcove of the art deco King Alfred leisure center on the Hove promenade on a busy January Wednesday morning, I have come out of the shadows. I am proud.

The comments from posting this set of images have been really nice to hear — how great I look and how fabulous the swimsuits look on me. Even when we have done a lot of self-development and soul searching and have worked hard on strengthening our internal validation rather than relying on external, it is undeniably a boost to our self-confidence when we are given a compliment. That is, if we are able to receive them. At times, when our self-worth is at a low point, we can't always hear them, accept them, believe them. We think the person is just making small talk or feels they ought to say something nice. Or maybe they are buttering us up because they want something from us. Or we believe that they mean it, but we can't see how they can possibly see us in that way because we absolutely can't see it ourselves. But what will serve us is when we can genuinely accept a compliment but not rely on them to feel good in our skin.

Knowing our bodies are good regardless of how they look and what others think of them is where I am and where I want to help others get to because we are worth so much more than how we look. Whilst I am proud of my body because I have learned to appreciate it for what it can do, it is, at the end of the day, just the meat suit that carries my soul around. It is the vessel that enables me to do what lights me up, what sustains me, what brings me joy. The shell from which my soul shines when I fully embrace her and allow her to do so. For so many years I didn't, so now I am making up for lost time.

What I have realized is that my value and strength are in owning my quiet power. Certain people in my life recognize the passion I have within me, which comes out when I talk about women and girls who have been told all their lives that their bodies are not good enough, who then learn that they are so much more than a body, and begin to see their worth is not held in how long their eyelashes are, or how many wrinkles they have, or what the numbers on the scales or tape measure say. I have only relatively recently fully accepted my introverted nature as a gift. I know I don't have to shout my passion and messages loudly from the rooftops. I can make an impact by quietly sharing it with those who are called to listen. Shining my light isn't floodlights and disco balls — it's a string of pretty, sparkling, fairy illuminations.

About Claudine Nightingill-Rane

I am Claudine Nightingill-Rane and I live in Hove, Sussex, on the south coast of England with my husband, two children, and my doggo. When I am not coaching, writing, parenting, or wifeing, I can usually be found in the sea, on a yoga mat, or in my hammock in the garden, lost in a book.

My calling to write came from my desire to help others learn from the experiences I have had. I spent a good chunk of my life not feeling good enough — my body, my personality, my everything — and thus, dulling my light, hiding away and editing parts of me I thought weren't likable. But then I had a revelation that I didn't have to be liked by or attractive to everyone. And with that, the realization that if I accept I won't be everyone's cup of tea, I could be more me and, by default, the perfect cuppa for the right people. The same went for my body: when I realized there was an alternative to hating it and spending my life shrinking it and that it was possible to be beautiful without fitting the beauty standards we are told are required of us, my life changed. Sea swimming has enabled me to flow along this journey. Learning that the blocks in my way were created by me and learning to appreciate what my body does for me and allows me to do was a game changer. It enabled me to create a career combining my two passions: helping girls and women harness the healing power of the ocean and learn to accept themselves as they are — mind, body, and soul.

Other things I have a strong opinion on: feminism and equality, mental health, ocean pollution, cold-water swimming, wine, coffee, and dark chocolate with sea salt.

You can find me on the social channels @SeascapeBlue

On Falling Apart
and Feeling Again

Sometimes I imagine running into Andrew while I'm grocery shopping.

There I am, picking up every Gala apple, inspecting them for bruises before placing them in my cart, and I bump elbows with him.

I say, "Excuse me," look up, and there he is — tall, lanky, a head of brown, floppy hair, a dorky, doctor version of Tom Selleck in *Magnum P.I.*, but with a longer, more prominent nose.

This grocery store run-in would give me the chance to tell him how the one very simple and seemingly innocuous question he asked me in his office seven years ago changed the course of my life.

I would have the chance to tell him how I carry his question with me every day.

It's in the pocket of my favorite jeans.

It's written in green gel pen on a hot pink post-it on my desk.

It pops up in my iPhone reminders every morning at 9 a.m. like a message from the divine.

It's also nestled in the back corner of my heart.

Yah. It's always with me.

* * *

I spent several years with Andrew.

No. He wasn't my lover (although I have to admit, I did find his brain quite sexy).

He was our couples' therapist.

S and I met with Dr. G every Wednesday morning at 10 a.m. for what felt like 105 years (it was more like six) before he retired in June of 2018.

* * *

If I close my eyes, I can still see everything in his tiny, three flights up, beige-themed therapy office — the brown leather couch on the back wall that went unused, although many mornings I wished I could close my eyes and take a quick nap to avoid all the hard stuff that would inevitably surface in our 50 minutes together, the black and white photos of beach dunes in Truro, Massachusetts (where I later learned from our mutual massage therapist he retired — and no, I haven't stalked him, although I've thought about it, naturally), and the Pothos plant that reminded me of *Little Shop of Horrors*, that weaved and stretched its long, green tendrils over his bookcases and desk, tirelessly hauling itself towards the light of the oversized window much like my toddler would reach for the organic, non-Oreos that I hid in the back of the highest kitchen cabinet.

* * *

Andrew was kind and patient and direct.

So, maybe I shouldn't have been surprised when he asked me his pointed question that rocked my world six years ago and continues to reverberate through my current reality.

You see, I was done.

Done with the fighting.

Done with the icy standoffs.

Done with the late-night crying-on-the-cold-bathroom-floor sessions.

And I finally declared it out loud during one of our Wednesday morning sessions in October of 2015.

"I want a divorce. And I have a lawyer."

And then Andrew dropped his bomb.

* * *

If this story were a movie and you were watching it at your local theater with a bucket of buttery popcorn in your lap, I would want to be played by Charlize Theron.

S would be played by Javier Bardem (I didn't ask S who should play him, I just want to be married to Javier Bardem in my movie. And ... it's my movie ... so ...).

And just to be clear, we don't even remotely resemble either of these actors.

Let me set the stage.

S and I met at a club in NYC.

S owned the club, and I was invited by my dearest, oldest childhood friend, Molly (that's her real name, and she would be played by Molly herself because Molly can act).

I spent the first part of the evening dancing on tables and drinking champagne with Molly.

I spent the latter part of the night nestled at the bar, talking to S about our families and our lives and also making out with him. He was a good kisser.

S was smart.

He did the *New York Times* crossword puzzle.

He was a lawyer before he was a bar owner.

He was one of three kids.

He was handsome and kind and had a very big, gap-toothed smile and a scruffy beard.

He loved music.

And he talked a lot (still does).

We were both dating other people.

It didn't matter.

Six months later, we were engaged to be married.

Two months later, we moved to Tokyo for S's work (he went back to lawyering).

Seven months later, we were married.

Nineteen months later, we welcomed to the world our first of three kids.

Three years later, we had three kids under four, a mortgage.

And fourteen years after meeting in an NYC club, we are sitting in Andrew's office and I'm dropping the divorce bomb.

It happened fast.

As life does, especially in movies.

* * *

"What do you *really* want, Natalie?"

This was the first question he asked me after I announced the attainment of my lawyer and the fact that I was done.

(But hold tight. It's not the question that ripples through my every day.)

This was my answer:

A condo in the center of town.

Someone to shovel the snow and mow the lawn and empty the dishwasher.

Someone to help with the kids and play with them when I was too tired.

Probably a lover.

Yes, definitely a lover.

And then Andrew dropped the *real* bomb — the question that pops up on my iPhone reminders every morning at 9 a.m.

"Natalie, how do you want to *feel*?"

I stumbled.

My mind went blank.

I searched for words.

I had none.

Feeling? What's that?

I was stumped.

So, we sat in silence (I always hated this — when your therapist just sits there and waits for you to come up with something to say), and then something magical happened.

I took a deep breath, closed my eyes, and my imagination took over.

I began to paint the picture in my mind of what happiness looked like to me.

And it looked like this in my mind:

I am standing at the stovetop, wooden spoon in hand, stirring a pot of my family's ragu — my grandmother's recipe that uses shredded carrots instead of sugar for a little sweetness.

Jerry Garcia is playing "The Way You Do the Things You Do" through the speakers in our kitchen. Our three kids are dancing wildly, tossing their bodies around and laughing in the kitchen.

And the holy grail of this movie scene that's playing out in my head is when S comes up behind me, pours me a glass of red wine, places it next to me, and then wraps his arms around my waist. He drops his head and rests it on my neck. I can feel the tickle of his beard hairs. He kisses me gently in that place behind my ear that makes all of the hair on my body stand up.

I opened my eyes, and it all poured out — tears, and in between the crying, these words:

I want to feel loved.

I want to feel adored.

I want to feel seen.

I want to feel taken care of.

I want to relax.

I want lightness and playfulness.

I want connection.

I want intimacy and coziness and sweetness.

I want time together.

I kept my head down, afraid to meet S's gaze.

I was embarrassed by the softness of my share.

I wanted to run. I wanted to hide. I wanted to barf into the rubbish bin in the corner of Andrew's office.

And this is why:

I was born the youngest of three kids and the only girl. I pushed hard to be the fastest, the strongest, the whatever-est of whatever thing I was striving for — just like my brothers. Gold stars, blue ribbons, invitations to your guys-only ski weekends. Sign me up. I wanted it all.

And most of the time, I got it.

Because I pushed.

I strived.

I excelled.

I made it happen for myself, by myself.

I had that *take-no-prisoners, get outta my way, I can do it all and win all the big prizes* kind of energy.

And I took that powerful energy into my life and my marriage.

I never asked for help.

I mowed the lawn seven months pregnant.

I learned how to drill through brick so I could build shelves in our garage.

I cooked homemade organic meals for my family — no sugar — every damn day.

I taught yoga to kids, worked at a local food pantry and made my kids the politest ones in the neighborhood (or at least I tried).

I was moving so damn fast, I didn't know what I really wanted, and I definitely had no idea how I wanted to *feel*.

Several years later, I was sitting in Andrew's office.

Numb. Overwhelmed. On a cocktail of antidepressants and anti-anxiety meds and wanting to run away from *all of it*.

* * *

S took my hand and moved his chair closer to mine.

He lifted my chin and looked me in the eyes.

"I want to give you all of that. Please let me."

I wish I could wrap this story up with a beautiful (all-natural, organic, jute) bow, but I won't do that. After all, this isn't really a 90-minute movie. And I'm not really Charlize Theron.

The past seven years have been a messy and winding journey of unraveling, unbecoming, and remembering what it means to *feel* again.

I've had to ask for help (this is the hardest).

I've had to communicate how I'm feeling to S, even when it's embarrassing.

I've had to let go of relationships where I couldn't show up with *all* of me.

I've had to learn how to say no to things — even when I know I can do them, but I know in my heart they will exhaust me.

I've had to let go of my perfectionism and my desire to *get it right* all the time.

I've had to learn how to process my rage, anger, grief, and sadness in safe ways.

I've had to learn how to trust myself and know deep in my bones that I matter, my feelings matter, what I *want* matters.

And NO, my marriage isn't all rainbows and unicorns. We still fight.

My kids aren't perfect. They have sh*t. Every human does. And parenting is the hardest job on the planet.

But life is a little sweeter when you allow yourself to slow down and feel again.

So, if you have a post-it and a pen handy, write this down:

"How do I want to feel today?"

Then stick it on your laptop, on your bathroom mirror, on the dashboard of your car.

And as often as you can, check back in with yourself.

How am I feeling right now and how do I *want* to feel?

Adjust your life accordingly.

And let me know how it goes. I'm always up for connection.

Love,
Natty

About Natty Frasca

Natty Frasca is a Life Coach and Wild Guide to Women Who Want MORE.

She lives with her three wild teenagers, hubby, two dogs, and a bunny outside of Boston, Massachusetts. And nothing turns her on more than teaching women how to live lives they are thrilled to wake up to.

Dear You, Dear Me

Have you ever met someone and instantly knew you were meant to meet? I have. With one friend in particular, it was like she was an answer to my prayers, and I drew her to me. A few months after we met, something happened that neither of us could have expected, and it shook our relationship. It was in the days afterward, during a group writing session for this book, that this letter came to me.

The me of months before would have seen the entire situation and experience through a different lens, but the me that was experiencing what had occurred saw it soooo differently. While I knew I hadn't been my best version with her in this particular instance, at my core, I knew all was ok, all was calm. I was seeing this all unfold from a perspective that showed her as the mirror she was for me. This perspective forced me to see the deep hurt I had not only caused her but other people in my life as well as myself. All those years before this, I hadn't been able to see it. I wrote the letter below, never expecting to share it, but the next evening my friend and I met and spoke in person, which was the first time ever (in this lifetime) that I had a girlfriend meet me and talk things out with me after a fight.

I didn't grow up knowing fighting was ok and healthy, and, in this moment, I was reminded of how special this friend was because I had finally drawn to me someone who would give me the opportunity to apologize. After I said my peace, this beautiful soul shared with me that the night before (just hours after I had written this letter), she decided to take a salt bath to detox and heal from this experience. Upon feeling she was done, she told me she went to get up and couldn't; she felt pulled back into the tub. In that instant, she said she had a vision of two beings bathed in bright white light with robes on and wreaths around their heads. She "immediately sensed it was our Essential (Higher) Selves directing and honoring our healing process, as they nodded and high-fived each other in satisfaction of the lessons learned and forgiveness achieved (forgiveness of each other and of themselves)." I stared at her in amazement and proceeded to read her this letter.

Sharing the part above feels profound because it shows my connection with her and hers with me, which further highlights each of our connections to one another and how deeply we are connected to everything. I believe this experience can bring awareness to how we draw people and situations into our lives, and no matter how it turns out, our Essential Selves are ecstatic at the results. We are ever-growing, constantly evolving, and involving beings of consciousness. I'm grateful to have learned from a dear friend and soul sister and am blessed she entered my life just as I had been praying for her. While a part of me still wishes this hadn't happened, that thought doesn't get far because I know our Essential Selves got together long before we arrived here and plotted this exact opportunity for massive growth to enter our lives.

I'm grateful for the magical workings of the Universe and the beautiful, sometimes heartbreaking, but always incredibly humbling (if we're able to look beyond ourselves) moments that make up our lives and remind us of the profound connection we have with each other and all that surrounds us. If you find yourself reading this, I pray you not only see yourself in the shadow of this letter but also the light. If you would allow it, I pray that I may be your mirror here and that this is the entry point, the piercing through the veil, the gateway for your soul to your journey of awakening, remembering, and returning to the truth of your own light. What was once seen as a mistake can now be seen as an opportunity to practice and refine.

Our light never goes out and can never be dulled or dimmed. Our perspectives are what fog up and distort our vessel that our light shines through and from. With each new opportunity to evolve and involve, our perspective shifts, and the vessel is cleared so that more and more of our light can be seen and felt by those around us. May this letter be one that shifts your perspective and clears your vessel so that you, too, can shine more of your beautiful, bright light into the world.

Dear You, Dear Me,

It's no surprise I hurt you.

I have been hurting you my whole life.

I have rejected you and despised you.

I have hated you and hidden you.

I have been ashamed of you and oftentimes sought to keep you a secret.

I have denied you and silenced you.

All of this has caused me to do and be all of these things to not only you, but to me as well.

You see ...

I am you. And you are me.

All I have done to you, I have also done to myself.

You are the pieces I have always wanted to accept about myself but have never felt worthy of.

And so, I sabotage you and the idea of a transparent, accepting, aligned relationship with you.

Out. Of. Fear.

Out of fear I allowed my EGO to rule me.

Out of fear I played in the shadows.

Out of fear I was unable to see a way out.

Out of fear I let you play in the shadows with me.

Up until now.

Up until now this is how it has been.

This has been the pattern.

"Stay small. Worry. Pay no mind to what doesn't feel right.

You're not selfish."

What a liar the small self is.

No more.

From this moment, I choose to see, think, hear, feel, and act as my Essential Self.

I call it in, my essence.

And in that, I choose to see you as YOUR Essential Self as well.

Nothing ever done can deny this aspect of myself.

Nothing done can ever deny this aspect of you.

This is who we really are.

Each Essential Self comes from the same Source.

I am you. And you are me.

I am deeply sorry for the distorted stories I bought into when I was playing small. I am deeply sorry for the pain I caused you when I was playing small.

My Essential Self knows all is well and all will continue to be well.

Under the emotional current, I can feel the calm.

I sense it and know it is there.

All is well with my Essential Self and with yours.

I accept this calm as my true nature and yours too.

As I am you and you are me.

I had no idea how my playing small hurt you.

My smallness feeds yours and yours feeds mine.

Because I am you and you are me.

What I do to myself, I do to you.

And so here it is:

I can't deny you anymore.

As I claim peace for myself, I claim it for you, too.

I release the shame.

I come out of hiding.

I step up and into my wholeness so you can do the same.

If my smallness causes you pain, then I know my being big will cause us each to rise. As I step out of the shadows, I shine my light for all to see.

My doing this releases you from the shadows and gives you permission to shine your light as well (not that you needed my or anyone else's permission!).

For I am you and you are me.

My love for you comes from a place deep, now.

A place where I choose to honor you and your soul, where I see you for who you really are: you are me.

You deserve to unapologetically shine and bravely be let out of the box and shown off with genuine self-assuredness.

I am capable of this now as I receive you as the gift from the Universe you are, as a blessing and beautiful part of me mirroring to me all the joy and unconditional love available in every moment.

I no longer feel the negative emotions.

I no longer think the negative thoughts about you.

For I know who you are.

I find worth in myself because of who I now know myself to be and thus I am now able to see the worth in you.

For you are me and I am you.

In honor of wholeness. In honor of love.

As one.

I am grateful for you.

I am grateful for our journey.

Thank you for being my mirror.

With courage, In love, out of the shadows and into the light.

In this moment and always,

In gratitude,

From the me in you and the you in me.

About Heather Robbins

Heather Robbins is originally from Zionsville, Indiana. She received a B.A. in philosophy from Indiana University and went on to receive her Doctorate in Physical Therapy from the University of Miami in Florida. After graduating, it wasn't long before Heather found herself fascinated by energy and became a certified High Speed Healing energy practitioner. Her soul purpose has been to educate her clients on energetics and the power of their thought patterns and belief systems. It is her life's purpose to empower souls to take their power back so they may bravely and unapologetically walk through each day spiritually aligned with their soul's original blueprint and purpose. It is her belief that when this is done, a person's inner light is able to shine brightly for all to see. Heather currently lives in Northern Virginia with her two beautiful children and loving husband.

www.wayshowerwellness.org

Loneliness

How do we truly know who our most authentic self is?

Loneliness

No influence from others

No fear of judgment

Loneliness

To sit with our thoughts, emotions, ideas, and fully perceive ourselves as a whole

Loneliness

About Madeline Myers

Madeline Myers, 17, daughter of Carrie Myers. An arising senior in high school, trying to discover the path meant for her in life in order to fulfill her dream of happiness and all-around fulfillment. The small things in life are what mean the most to her, from sunbathing to baking for her loved ones. Being included in this collaborative book means a lot to her as the women in this book are beyond inspiring to her through their growth and self-perseverance. If she could tell her younger self one thing, it would be to unapologetically be yourself, regardless of how others perceive or react.

Instagram: @madelinem1863

People-Pleaser in Recovery

I am an Adult Child of an Alcoholic (ACOA), which means I grew up in a home that often felt dysfunctional, unpredictable, and invalidating due to my family members' substance abuse. It also means that I became overly sensitive to the needs of others in an attempt at self-preservation. There is an undeniable link between relational trauma and people-pleasing. Due to the complexities of the trauma that I experienced growing up and in adulthood, my cost-benefit analysis perception(s) became skewed. In some ways, it was emotionally safer for me to simply say "yes" even when I wanted to say "no." "Yes" often meant peacekeeping, while "no" meant chaos and uncertainty. "Yes" was my method of control.

The combination of uncertainty and a sense of powerlessness over my own experiences were the breeding ground for being a yes-woman. That became my identity. For many years and into my adulthood, I didn't realize that this behavior was problematic. In fact, I saw it as morally upstanding. I was someone who cared, someone who helped. Someone who was unselfish. I can see now that I was someone who was completely disconnected from myself. Frankly, I had no idea how to truly care for my own needs, let alone identify them. Ignoring my intuitive sense in lieu of pleasing and rescuing others led me down multiple paths where I did not belong. The relationship with my mother, perhaps, was the most notable and life-altering of all.

My mother had a long history of trauma, chronic and severe mental illness, and substance abuse. At the end of her life, she suffered greatly with alcohol addiction and a descent into a severity of mental illness she'd never been before. I, therefore, suffered greatly with co-dependency, ambiguous grief, and crippling anxiety. I sensed that the end of her life was near. Being unable to predict exactly when and how she would pass was excruciating. She was not taking care of herself, barely eating, not bathing, and her house was a complete disaster area. There were times when she claimed she could not walk and was crawling to the restroom. Whether her inability to walk was a physical malady or delusion, it was real to her. She spun into paranoia and panicked often. Sometimes, she experienced hallucinations. In her reality, children were hiding in baskets, misplacing items in her home, and torturing her when her back was turned.

In those times, she called me for comfort. If you've ever tried to comfort an intoxicated, irrationally panicked, and deeply traumatized human, you know what an undertaking that is. If you haven't, imagine that you've been tasked with slowing down a runaway train. The situation defies your understanding of logic, kickstarts your entire being into fight-or-flight, and creates a looming sense of impending doom.

The difference between a runaway train and my mother, aside from the obvious, was history. At least with a runaway train, I could detach and find some semblance of comfort in *trying* to stop it. If it ended in disaster, that would certainly be devastating, but I was still separate from the train. With my mom, I experienced a desperation to help her that segued into co-dependency. Who could possibly leave their own mother in the depths of their suffering? She was not okay, so I was not okay. Much like she did, I lived in a state of fear and illness.

Furthermore, I was aware of the varying traumas she experienced in childhood and adulthood. It seemed that there was no kind of abuse she hadn't suffered at some point in her lifetime. On top of that, I'd witnessed the Universe deal her tough hand after tough hand throughout my own life. I deeply empathized with her because I knew her to be sweet, kind, and nurturing. She was a stay-at-home caretaker and there was quite literally never a time when she was not there for me. She loved her kids more than herself, was a creative soul, loved mystery shows and rock music. For a long time, it was impossible for me to find a "fair" reason to justify setting firm boundaries with her. She had not meant to hurt me, after all. She was deeply hurting herself.

All the same, I began to associate my interactions with her with terror as time went on. Whenever she called me, I answered with shaking hands and heart palpitations. I never knew what the phone call would bring. When she requested me to pick up goods for her, I obliged despite the pit in my stomach signaling that I was likely walking into pain. Looking back, in those last few years of her life, there wasn't a visit that did not traumatize me. She fell often, spoke in nonsensical phrases, and accused me of wrong-doings. She was in denial of the severity of her mental and physical state, and no amount of my tears, pleading, or panic would change her mind.

One visit stands out to me in particular. It was the visit in which my body finally said "no" for me, because I would not. Ironically, this visit was arranged by me, as I wanted to pick up some photographs that I knew she kept in photobooks. My plan was to create a scrapbook for my younger brother, who was serving in the Navy and out at sea at the time. I was excited to do something kind for him. I was even more excited when I called my mom that morning at around 8 a.m. to share my idea with her — she seemed clear-headed, was engaged, and even sounded like the Mom I knew! It was a beautiful, blue-skies, Midwest day, and my spirits were uncharacteristically high as I drove the hour-long trip to her home, the childhood home I once knew so well.

When I got there, I climbed the steep steps up to the front door. My optimism quickly faded as a familiar sense of dread flooded through me. I heard loud music playing and my blood ran cold. I knew what this meant. She was drunk. With shaking hands, I knocked on the door. No answer. I tried again, panic rising with every knock. Why wasn't she answering? What if she was passed out? Stuck somewhere? How did she go from coherent to drunk so quickly, and so early in the day? What if I walked in and found her dead?

It was then that I noticed the handle on her screen door was broken. In a state of dissociation, I drove to the local dollar store and purchased a screwdriver, drove back to the home, and began the process of breaking into the house. As I was doing so, I heard a scream followed by a crash from inside. In a cloud of rising desperation, I broke open the door to find my mother half sprawled on the floor, laughing and clinging to a nearby lampstand. How could she possibly find humor in this? I'm dying inside and she thinks this is funny? I was enraged.

She stood up and I asked her what in the hell was going on through gritted teeth. She laughed again and spoke gibberish. She leaned on me, her weight swaying and my shoulders caving. Her eyes were glazed, and her breath smelled of cheap vodka. It was clear that she could not walk on her own. In that moment, nearly 30 years of suppressed emotion came out. My body took full control and I screamed at her. I pleaded with her to get it together. I cried, furious and feral and despondent. She was shocked at my response and fell back into her chair, curled into the fetal position and fell asleep shortly after. I ran out of the house and sobbed in my car. It was that day that I accepted that I could no longer set my needs aside for the benefit of others. It was then that I realized I was killing my own spirit in a meager yet earnest attempt to save someone else's. Love led me into this mess, and love would lead me out. Self-love. I had to set boundaries. I had to start saying "no."

My people-pleasing did not heal until I took an honest look at my own role in my relational traumas, objectively and without shame. In doing so, I realized that if I had set boundaries earlier, I would have avoided direct exposure to deeply traumatic experiences. In retrospect, those around me had tried to steer me away from those co-dependent behaviors, but I refused to listen. People-pleasing did not cease until I started prioritizing my own needs, thereby exposing myself to the pain of letting others down. This allowed me to recognize that I could hold pain, that pain is manageable, and that I simply could not protect others from their own pain. I had to learn that I wasn't saving others — I was assassinating myself. Eventually, with practice, I was able to detangle others' pain from my own and begin the noble work of tending to it.

Co-dependency cannot live in a healthy body, mind, or spirit. Let's get really honest here: "People-pleasing" is just a prettier term for "co-dependent." Chronic co-dependency leads to resentment and, as Dr. Gabor Mate, author of *When the Body Says No*, says, "Resentment is soul suicide." I did not truly heal until I made a commitment to make an authentic return to my true self. Healing began with "I love you and I love me, but *my* job is to *take care of myself only."*

It took me nearly three decades to uncover my own truths. Everything is as it should be. For me. For you. For them. I don't call the shots of the Universe; I just exist in it. I have to accept that there is pain in the world for myself and for others. More importantly, I have to remember that it isn't my fault. Truthfully, if I fix everything, then I rob everyone — self-included — of the priceless opportunity of expansion and growth. I cannot be a savior to others. In fact, it is quite grandiose of me to take that duty upon myself. Utopia is for the afterlife and we're not there yet.

My mother is no longer earthside, and I am still healing from our shared experiences. The unbreakable thread that ties us together reminds me that she never wanted harm for me. She sends me butterflies, pennies, and heart symbols to remind me that I am whole and worthy as I am. I grieve her loss, and I celebrate the peace she has found in the afterlife. She's making pancakes from scratch and jamming out to hard rock, laughing all the while. I know that in her wellness, she would have given anything to spare me an ounce of pain. Today, I use that knowledge to gain a sense of comfort rather than a sense of guilt.

I am a people pleaser in recovery. I engage in regular therapy as well as a daily commitment to prioritize my wellness before all else. I no longer allow myself to be agreeable in order to avoid my feelings or the discomfort of my grander reality, nor anyone else's. I gave it up in exchange for the gifts of peace and empowerment; if you relate at all to my experience, I hope that you will too.

About Laura Butts

Laura Butts is a complex trauma survivor and mental health advocate located near St. Louis. She received a Master of Social Work degree from the University of Illinois at Urbana-Champaign in 2015 and is now a licensed clinical social worker and mental health therapist. She is especially passionate about maternal mental health, spiritual wellness, and healing generational trauma. Laura loves researching alternative, creative therapy modalities and incorporating them into her healing practices.

When Laura isn't at her therapy practice, you can find her enjoying time with her partner and their growing family, creating art of all kinds, or spending time in nature. Her toddler, mini-Labradoodle, and German Shepard keep her hands full!

This is Laura's first contribution to a published piece. She is looking forward to authoring more works centered around healing and spiritual themes in the future. For updates as well as more relatable and inspiring content, keep up with Laura on her Instagram:
@laura.in.good.faith.

From Victim to Victorious

Complete. Triumphant. Confident. Assured. Relaxed. Clear.

Grounded, from the soles of my feet to the crown of my head, through the core of my very being.

Radiant. I feel golden light shimmer and shine in and through my eyes, through my words, emanating from my heart and radiating throughout my body ... this I know is the undeniable, eternal and infinite grace of The Source of All Things that animates me and all things. I feel the Power of Love pour through me like warm golden honey, guiding my thoughts, my words, and my actions, from doubt to knowing, from insecurity to security, from fear to faith.

Gratitude is my only response. Immense, overwhelming GRATITUDE.

My breath is suddenly caught short as the totality of my existence dawns within my consciousness, sending hot, wet tears down my cheeks. Sobbing, I sink to my knees on my yoga mat, slowly I crawl forward into child's pose, bowing to GRACE, my third eye making contact with the mat and, in that moment, connecting me to a larger, infinitely powerful me ... connecting me to all that is, was, and ever will be. In that moment, everything makes sense. I finally understand that all the years of heartache, insecurity, depression, anger, and isolation, all the minor and major tragedies that I had experienced in my life, had a purpose. I understand that it was I, in fact, that chose those experiences, that chose those teachers, that chose those lessons. In this moment of Eternal Connection, I understand that I am not separate from those that hurt me, that there is only Love, and that the only response to fear, anger, hate, and yes, even violence is Love. The Power of Love to heal all wounds, transform all things, and illuminate all darkness, is undeniable. In this moment, I realize that I would not know this truth if I hadn't experienced years of judgment, criticism, abandonment, doubt, disconnection, self-judgment, and self-hate. I now understand, for myself and all others, that the pain that we experience in life is the catalyst for our divine connection.

At 55 years, almost 56, I have finally surrendered. I have finally surrendered, fully and completely, to the life I have lived, am living right now in this present moment, and to the future moments that I have yet to experience. Suddenly, the phrase "Let go and Let God" not only rings true, but I now understand it to be the only truth there is.

I have surrendered to a childhood of consistent criticism for every aspect of my being. I have surrendered to a lack of love, affection, acceptance, approval, and validation for the miracle that, as a child, full of wonder for the world, I knew myself to be. I have surrendered to the belittlement, judgment, and abandonment that was shown to me by my parents and siblings alike. I have surrendered to all the moments when, as a child and a young adult, I desperately sought loving guidance, wise words, and validation but was met with only indifference, gossip, and betrayal.

Through the conscious act of surrender, I have been transformed. As I gave up the fight to understand others, I learned that the only thing that I needed to understand was myself. Through the years of counseling, bodywork, yoga, and meditation, I discovered the beauty and talents within me as I gradually let go of the grip I had on those that had hurt me. Surrender blossomed into gratitude, slowly and beautifully, like a rosebud opening day by day, in the light of Divine Truth.

I have nothing but gratitude for an adolescence of self-doubt and yearning, for the depression, self-hate, and eventually anger at a family that refused to see me, for it was the darkness of those years that drove me to seek happiness and understanding of myself. I have nothing but gratitude for my young adult years, during which I sought, and found, my own healing through the acknowledgment of my own truths. I learned that I could CHOOSE how others affected me, and that their assumption that they were "better" than me was simply the reflection of their own insecurities.

During all those years and decades, the Sacred Spark within me, and all things, never went out. What I didn't receive from my family, I learned to seek through my own experiences. As a child, I spent endless hours outside, by myself, walking through the fields and pine forests near my New England home. I went on magical bike rides on country roads lined with giant maple trees, the October sun streaming through their brilliant scarlet and orange leaves. And in the winter, I went ice skating on a frozen pond in the woods behind a small dairy farm next door. The trees bare, the sun occasionally peeking through thick grey clouds as I practiced my back cross-over and spins, struggling to keep my fingers warm in my gloves. Surrounded by the trees, shrubs and grasses, streams and boulders, clouds, birds, and rabbits, I instinctively knew that I was always safe, protected, and deeply loved. I was never judged, criticized, or made fun of. Instead of constantly doubting myself, my times alone in Nature taught me to trust my instincts, to trust something strong and clear within me that was far more powerful than just "me."

At a very young age, perhaps two or three, I became aware that, in the eyes of my father, I was not as "good" or capable as my older sister. When I learned how to read at the age of four, I retreated into a world of books, fascinated by stories and myths of faraway lands. I was insatiably curious about the world I found myself in and would read up to 20 books a week, eventually making my way through the entire young adult and science fiction sections at the East Longmeadow Public Library. I had a coin bank that was a small globe, and as I read about different countries, cultures, and customs, I would dream about the countries I would visit and live in someday.

My curiosity about life blossomed into a full-blown love of science, and although school was easy for me, and I was an A student, I really didn't know I was smart and had a level of comprehension and academic ability that is rare in this world. I was continually criticized and ignored by my father, who put all hopes and dreams into my older sister, and affection towards my younger sister. As the middle daughter, I was considered to be both physically and academically inferior to both of my sisters, and any achievements that I had were challenged or routinely ignored.

By the time I turned 16, any self-esteem that I had completely collapsed. In my quest to have a body that was acceptable by 1980s standards, I became anorexic and then bulimic. I dove into extreme depression during my senior year of high school.

I finished my senior classes at home, I went into isolation, and I didn't go to my senior prom or graduation ceremony. I truly believed there was something wrong with me, and my parents and siblings, all deeply mired in their own experiences of dysfunction and survival, only offered confirmation that there was something wrong with me, by the way I have been treated since birth.

While I had truly transformational experiences both in and out of the classroom in college, traveled to Europe and

Japan, and spent almost three years in South America as a Peace Corps Volunteer, I was still desperately searching for the love and validation that I had never received as a child. Despite my education and accomplishments, I struggled to see my value; I struggled to believe that I was worthy of love or success at any level. I married at 26, and after I gave birth to my daughter at age 27, I knew that if I didn't understand what happened to me and why I felt so unhappy with myself, that I would be raising her with the same feelings of disempowerment, self-judgment, and self-criticism that I knew so well. A friend introduced me to Re-Evaluation Counseling, also known as Co-Counseling. It was the first time that I learned, after 15 grueling years, that it was possible to feel differently about myself.

In January of 1994, with my year-old baby girl, I left my husband and moved to Boulder, Colorado, with friends to practice RC Therapy. I sought, and then found, happy, positive, confident people that understood the power of personal transformation through counseling, breathwork, bodywork, and yoga. I learned from them how to nurture and strengthen my own connection to the Sacred Spark that I had felt as a child, what I had come to experience again as the Divine Light and Truth of Love within myself. I sought and then found the self-worth and self-love within myself. I now know that self-worth and self-love are not feelings that can ever be given by another, by a parent, by siblings, by lovers, partners, or spouses, but are Eternal Truths that we can only experience when we understand that it is we, no other, that continue to inflict our wounds by claiming our victimhood. When we find the courage to be 100% honest about the degree of trauma that we experienced, we can release the shame, guilt, and anger that we have been repressing for having been the object of someone else's victimization. When we truly acknowledge our pain, we release the story that we have been holding in our bodies, telling ourselves over and over that we are wounded, that we are victims. When we release the pain of the past, our physical bodies change, allowing us to become conscious of who we really are in the present moment.

One day in a powerful counseling session, I finally said what I had been afraid to admit all those years, that I didn't think my father loved me. In that moment of truth-telling, my perception of myself radically shifted — from blaming myself for not being good enough to having compassion for myself for the lack of love and emotional abuse that I had experienced. It wasn't MY FAULT that I wasn't shown love, affection, or encouragement. In fact, the way I was treated had absolutely nothing to do with me or my inherent worth but had everything to do with how my father had been treated as a child. I learned that my father had been considered "the least favorite son" by his parents and siblings and had experienced severe physical and emotional abuse throughout his life. Hurt people will and do hurt people, and in my case, like in most families, it is the innocent children that become caught up in the cycle of dysfunction. This has and will continue from one generation to the next until someone has the courage it takes to heal the cycle of victimhood and transgenerational trauma. Centuries of abuse and abandonment, supported by religions that teach abuse and abandonment as punishments for "original sin" and inherent "unworthiness," have resulted in a cruel and dysfunctional world that blames and shames victims for the abuse and trauma that they experience.

I learned that my eating disorder was the way I coped with continuous yet subtle emotional abuse. I realized that despite the years of feeling worthless, unattractive, and utterly lost in a world that I did not agree with, that I was a survivor and that I did the very best I could with everything I had. Over the years, self-doubt and insecurity shifted to admiration for my courage and willingness to challenge the demeaning views that my family continued to project on me. After all, who gave them the right to judge me? Apparently, I did. By accepting their view of me as my own, by giving my power away, I had allowed my father and my family to determine my worth. As long as I wasn't in control of my thoughts and feelings, I was incapable of changing my addictive thoughts and behavior. I had realized that I had internalized the judgment and criticism that I grew up with, and it wasn't until I took responsibility for what I thought of myself that I was able to change my inner dialogue from self-criticism and self-hate to recognizing my self-worth and then being able to act from a place of self-love.

The unshakeable power of our own knowing, self-worth, and self-love can only come to us through its absence. Believe it or not, it is no one else's job to give us self-worth and self-love, for what they give, they can and surely will take away. It is only when we have the courage to surrender the opinions and criticisms of others that we can move from seeing ourselves as a victim to stepping into the divine reality of our lives as empowered and victorious.

About Medea Galligan, MS Nutrition, CHHC AADP RYT

Through the process of learning how to connect to a force that runs through ALL THAT IS, I learned how to become present in my physical body. I learned what the true lessons of yoga are and what strength, balance, and flexibility actually mean, not just as physical benefits but as a way of BEING from one present moment to the next. After 12 years of study and practice, I completed a yoga teacher training program, which illuminated my path to my power as a woman, a teacher, and as a healer. Since that time, I have been honored to guide my students toward the numerous benefits and transformative power of gentle, restorative, and yin yoga, as well as meditation and Pranayama.

Through the use of ancient vibrations of the Universe, I learned how to hold sacred space for my students to connect to their Authentic Divine Selves, allowing the shift from loneliness, fear, guilt, shame, and self-judgment to deep forgiveness, eternal love, and radiant joy.

As a Functional Medicine Nutritionist, I help my clients understand and heal the root of their health imbalances and introduce yoga to my clients as a positive way of connecting to and loving their bodies. I incorporate private yoga classes in my personalized programs and am available for private and small group classes, and I also run The Golden Gate Yoga & Wellness Retreat Center. If you feel that I can support you on your journey to better health, deeper peace, and joy, please visit my website at www.MedeasHealthyLifestyleConcepts.com

Given Up for Adoption: A Conversation With My Younger Self

I was once asked, if I could meet my younger self now, what I would like her to know, what I would feel compelled to share with her from my more mature perspective, and I thought what a powerful question that was. And as I closed my eyes and imagined actually standing in front of my younger self and taking her hands in mine, I felt an unexpected rush of emotion welling up within me. The emotion of compassion, deep compassion as I became aware of her relative immaturity and her vulnerability, even as she stood proud and determined behind her guise of "being a young adult."

As she stood before me, she suddenly represented millions of other young women in the world as well, many of whom had "grown up" and had been encouraged, by parents and society at large, to put "childish" ways behind them, reign in their wild imaginations and fit into the mold that was in line with expectations that their parents and society had of them now that they had become "adults."

I wanted to hold all of their hands and, with great love and empathy, tell them that they were all beautiful and perfect just as they were, in all their glorious uniqueness and naivete, and just their very being here was their gift to the Universe. That there was no one in all of creation quite like them and that they didn't have to try and fit into a box or pretend to be someone that they weren't to please other people. They really didn't! That was just others projecting expectations onto them and their unconscious belief that they had to conform! I'd tell them that their open-heartedness and their vulnerability were to be treasured and honored as they continued to grow and mature into a deeper understanding of their true nature, not pushed aside and seen as weak. And last but by no means least, I would tell them the most powerful tenet of all, which is to *love themselves*.

Sadly though, I know that just hearing someone else saying it's important to love yourself is often not enough and that what I came to realize bringing up my own two children and caring for many others in my work is that it's the actual personal experience of love in action during their childhood and early adulthood that teaches them best what that word "love" really means. What love really feels like in the very core of your being. So, I would explain that if they didn't love themselves, it wasn't because they were unlovable, but because of their negative self-talk, probably programmed from childhood.

If the young infant is shown love consistently by caring and attentive parents, they begin to come to know their own self-worth, experience a positive feedback loop that grows and strengthens their personal identity, and they grow up knowing what inner contentment and security feel like. From this place that is free from fear and anxiety — two emotions that arise when the child doesn't feel understood or reassured —arises spontaneous feelings of joy and wellbeing, which are part of the experience of knowing love for yourself, and others, in its true fullness.

If my younger self expressed discomfort at the idea of loving herself, as it didn't feel like a very familiar concept for her, I would give her a big hug and gently explain that it wasn't her fault if she didn't realize how perfectly love-able she was exactly as she was and that it was a very good thing that we had identified that she hadn't been loving herself or accepting who she really was because it was never too late to start, and that it would be the best investment she ever made in herself.

As I imagine all of this, I write not just to my younger self now but to all of you beautiful, unique souls who may read these words.

Think of it this way. When we're born, we can be likened to a brand-new computer. Everything that we experience from day one on earth is programming us, as we absorb absolutely everything that we see, hear and experience like a sponge.

The reason I mention this is to remind us that the parenting we each experienced and the environment we found ourselves in were totally out of our control within the context of our "story" (although not from a soul's perspective, which many believe chose all the details of this incarnation through which to learn and evolve.)

And those early years, as we grew up and began exploring life as independent "adults," our view of the world and how we processed what we experienced — based on our programming and sense of self-worth — were shaped and influenced, to a large degree, on what others in our lives had passed on to us as their truth!

So, without realizing it, and thinking we humans are all pretty much the same, when we are young adults just venturing out independently from the family home, we often tend to compare ourselves with others around us, being our own worst critics and somehow managing to find ourselves lacking or not good enough in some way if we've not developed a healthy positive self-image.

The sad thing is it seems that everyone is doing this, including the people we're admiring who are comparing themselves to us! We might not see or recognize our own strengths and positive attributes because of our unconscious limiting self-beliefs or because we've never been encouraged to believe in ourselves, but others often do and find themselves wishing that they were more like us. What an irony! And rather sad, don't you think, that others might think more of us than we think of ourselves because of our programming or because we simply didn't know the power and authority we have to direct our thoughts in a positive and self-affirming way.

This is why deciding that loving ourselves is a priority from now on is a pivotal and life-transforming decision. When we start to treat ourselves with the love and care that we often extend to others and become our own best friend, that's when the true healing can begin; we can become masters of our lives and align with our souls' yearning for love and expansion.

When my youngest son was just three and a half, he looked at me earnestly one morning and said, "Mumma, love is all the people need." Wow, now where did that come from at such a tender age? He clearly hadn't been pondering the meaning of life and thinking about what people needed to be happy, and he didn't seem to be just repeating something he'd heard us say! Maybe because he hadn't long transitioned from the world of spirit into the world of form, it was his higher self's innate wisdom talking? It warmed my heart, that's for sure, and reminded me of the quote, "Wisdom oft comes from the mouth of babes."

My understanding is that our soul's urging is to remember our at-one-ment with our Source and that our real journey here is to become aware of that urge within and to let it guide us back into the awareness of the pure infinite love that is our birthright and our true nature.

So now, this evolved version of myself — with the insight and wisdom gained as I've navigated the peaks and troughs and dived deeply into esoteric wisdom and ancient knowledge passed down through the ages about the hero's journey and the inherent perfection in all of creation — I can sit with my younger self who is so sweet and earnest but deeply preoccupied with questions about who she is and the nature of reality. I can offer her this reassurance as my eyes well up with tears of deep compassion for the confusion and heartache that she has endured as her untamed ego mind has told her stories about herself that were simply not the truth.

I will tell her ... There are no mistakes in the Universe, dear sweet one. You ask why me? Why did I have to be given away for adoption? And my answer will be because it was your dharma, your purpose in life, what you were put here to experience and ultimately overcome. Cosmic law is perfect. Your soul chose your parents and the circumstances you would experience in this lifetime to learn self-love through the perceived experience of abandonment and rejection. The "story" is not "who" you are, and the journey is to awaken to that and come home to the truth of who and what you truly are — that is, a divine soul having a human experience here on earth in physical form because you're meant to be, and not because you were a random accident.

I will tell her that there really are no "accidents" and that I know in my heart of hearts that everything unfolds in perfect timing for our highest and greatest good.

Falling pregnant at 17 in the 1960's when you weren't married was definitely considered unacceptable — and especially when you were a Catholic teenager — so from a societal point of view, yes, the story of your mothers anguish and how you came to be here in physical form seems like a very sad story with a tragic outcome as she ran away to a mother and baby home to give birth to you and didn't tell her parents or two sisters that she was pregnant for fear of retribution.

I'll wrap my arms around her and hold her tight as she tells me that the story that she grew up with — that she was special and chosen — sounded kind of nice when she was little but began to loom like a shadow in the corner of her psyche as she matured and came to understand what being adopted really meant, as she saw a baby being born in her nursing training and she began to wonder endlessly about her biological origins and why it had happened to her.

I'll remind her that she was a kind, loving, and thoughtful young woman and that her confusion and introspection were totally understandable because she didn't realize then that there's an order and an infinite organizing intelligence that governs the Universe, and it's no wonder that she felt like fate had been unkind.

I'll remind her that she is so loved and that all the challenging times and painful soul searching takes her on a beautiful journey of self-discovery, and that all the while along the way, her higher self guides her in a multitude of ways — to read this book, meet that person, notice the still inner voice whispering, travel there, listen to that, apply for this — and she grows wise and confident, trusting that everything that happens to her is for her highest and greatest good.

And I'll reassure her that one day she understands that everything that happens to her is a gift for her transformation and that she comes to realize the many blessings that there were in being adopted. She begins to experience inner peace and deep gratitude and learns to accept that you can't change what is, so freedom from suffering lies in surrendering, and trusting that all is in divine and perfect order.

And then I'll gently tell her that by a series of synchronistic events and encounters, she does find and meet her birth mother in the not-too-distant future, and the narrative of abandonment and rejection that had defined her beginnings was not how it was at all! Quite the contrary, in fact. She *had* been loved, and her young mother really had wanted to keep her but being young and without resources, she had been unable to find a way.

I would reassure her that the burden of not knowing would be lifted, and she would, at last, see the whole picture from a higher perspective with no more judgment. That nothing is either good or bad, it simply is, and ultimately, it's our judgments and conceptualizing about it that cause us to suffer. Being called Geraldine Ann and then Sarah Jane didn't mean she wasn't "who" she was meant to be — in fact, her true essence was nameless, formless and perfect, whatever the story.

I imagine she'll smile broadly at me, suddenly radiating a new lightness of being as she takes a long, slow, deep breath and takes my hand in hers.

We'll burn some incense, light a candle, and sit together in silent meditation to give thanks for the eternal now moment, the Present, in which the lila of life in form plays out throughout the cosmos and we'll know that we're embedded within the whole, that this IS the perfection and love is all there is. And we'll laugh joyfully as we hug, and I remind her to trust that everything she experiences is a gift with hidden blessings that will become clear in the fullness of time ...

As I emerge from my reverie, a smile is born on my lips as I rest in the renewed knowing, deep within, that my soul said "yes" to it all so that it could shine ever brighter as it continues to grow and evolve through the chosen "individualized" story of "I am adopted, abandoned and unloved" towards a place of peaceful surrender and acceptance that "all is well."

I wonder, what would *you* like *your* younger self to know?

Here is a poem written by my eldest son when he was 24.

I'd like to offer this poem as a poignant reminder that life is full of blessings if only we choose to see them. To lift the energy of the reader who may have felt a bit emotional as they identified with the exchange with my younger self and invite them to focus on those times of joy and magic in their lives, practicing living in the moment with gratitude for what is and trusting that all is well and perfect just as it is.

My Cup Runneth Over

Have you ever felt like your heart could burst?
Like there was no way to quench life's loving thirst?
And you wanted to give everybody a hug,
Even if they then asked if you'd taken a drug ...
Have you ever been so delightfully satisfied,
That you got just that little bit teary-eyed?
Thinking, "Oh, this moment is just so delicious!
And I know for my soul it's extremely nutritious."
"The love that I'm feeling is almost too much,
I don't know if my little heart is big enough!"
Almost in an ecstatic trance,
And all you wanted to do was dance.
Your crew all around you having fun,
And you remember just how far you've come.
The people in your life are gems,
How lucky you are to have them as friends.
You're enjoying a little slice of bliss,
Thinking, "I must have done something right to deserve this!"
And the gratitude with which you were struck,
Was as if you'd swallowed an elixir of luck.
Those memories are golden, which makes sense, to be frank,
Because they're going to go straight into the memory bank.
You wouldn't sell that moment in time,
If someone offered you a million dollars, or a dime.

Because moments like that,

Have a worth you can't measure,

And are ultimately your greatest treasure.

And the fact that the magic happened there and then,

Proves to you that in the future, it can happen again.

So now, every morning, you wake in the knowing,

That such great possibility is always ongoing.

And you make sure to practice living in the moment,

Because presence and gratitude are essential components.

Then you'll really live, while you're alive,

And never forget that you're not just living to survive!

So when you witness those scenes, your heart as warm as wine,

When your smile's so broad and your eyes have a shine,

Look up at the sky as the moon's passing over,

Smile to yourself and say, "My cup runneth over!"

About Sarah Collinge

I qualified as a nurse at 21 and worked on surgical wards in the U.K. and abroad as well as in the regional burns unit in London. My mum was a nurse, and I later discovered my birth mother was a nurse and my birth father, uncle and grandfather were all doctors. Whilst in London, I entered a writing competition in a national magazine titled "Win A New Career." Asked to write about why I wanted a new career, I wrote about being adopted and the connection with the medical profession both in my biological ancestry and my upbringing, and mused at my decision to follow the same path. I had considered a change and looked at a beauty therapy course. I won that competition, and the prize was a beauty therapy course with Steiner International in London, whose course I had looked at. Destiny? Qualifying with distinction I now offer bespoke treatments in the home. I have two boys and eventually stopped nursing.

I love children, with a particular interest in baby care. I have been a sole charge baby nanny for the past three years and am presently completing my book, in which I share my tips and guidance for helping babies thrive in their first year. I am soon to train as a doula and offer consultations to support parents in that first challenging year.

To contact me to have a chat, confidentially and with no obligation, about how I might be of service to you either during pregnancy or after birth with your baby or your own self-care, or to talk about your adoption experience, you can find my details at: www.sarahcollinge.com

Soul Rejuvenation

I was working as a freelancer in marketing. I was over-worked and underpaid, always worrying about paying the bills and finding more work. I felt like a slave to the corporate world. I couldn't see a way out and felt so stuck.

In my heart, I knew I was completely overwhelmed and heading straight for burnout if things didn't change. There was no way I could continue a life of sleepless nights and endless dependency on caffeine and alcohol to get me through each day. The perpetual undercurrent of anxiety that I clung to like a safety blanket — as though it was actually my driving force — felt more alien than ever, yet the fear of not knowing how to function without it held me in its grip like a vice.

As a child, I'd always been interested in nature, the earth, her plants and animals. And I loved crystals, alternative therapies — anything that connected me with nature. But as an adult, I didn't know how or when the feeling of being so disconnected from myself and the natural world had started — or how it had gotten this far. I'd become so caught up in my work and self-imposed responsibility to others that I'd completely lost sight of what was important to me.

Before my career in marketing, I'd felt the pull to go deeper with my interest in the alternative healing modalities that had supported me so deeply in my personal life. I embarked on a journey of training professionally in holistic therapies, aromatherapy, plant medicine, and angelic Reiki. I set up my own practice but didn't have the business skills in the early days to make it work. My accidental career in marketing began to flourish when peers in my industry asked if I could help them with their social media marketing, as they loved the style and tone of voice of my brand and wanted help to craft their own.

It wasn't a conscious decision to step away from a career that I loved so much but I lived alone and with rent and bills to pay, so I took every marketing assignment that came my way. Before long, I was consumed by long days staring at a screen and a distant awareness of a waning connection to my true purpose. I adopted the mindset that this was just the way it was, and this was my job now. After all, I was good at it, but I'd never felt as ungrounded and disconnected. I'd get used to it, I thought.

One day, as I was scrolling through my Facebook feed, I saw an ad for a nature retreat. It looked like the perfect escape from my busy digital-heavy life. I clicked on the link and browsed through the website. They had a variety of retreats to choose from, but the one that caught my eye was the Women's Nature Retreat. The description said that it was a weekend getaway for women who wanted to reconnect with themselves and nature.

It felt like a sign. I knew I needed to go on this retreat. I felt the lost parts of myself calling to come home. It was the perfect opportunity to step away from my busy life and clear my head.

The day finally arrived, and I packed my bags, ready for a weekend of soul searching and nature connection. When I arrived at the retreat center, I was greeted by the other women who were attending. We all introduced ourselves and then went on a hike through the nearby forest. As we walked, we talked about our lives and the reasons why we had signed up for the retreat.

I felt a sense of deep belonging and sisterhood with these women, and I knew that we were all there for the same reason: to reconnect with ourselves and the natural world around us. To each remember our own inner true nature. I could feel my soul rejuvenating and an awareness that I'd allowed her to become so parched.

The next few days were spent exploring nature through a variety of activities, including hiking, foraging wild food, journaling, and sunset yoga. It was the most soul-nourishing experience I had ever had. By the end of the weekend, I felt refreshed, renewed, and connected to myself and nature in a way I hadn't before.

There is something special about the plants and herbs that grow around us everywhere we look. They have a way of connecting us to nature, and to the natural world. They have a way of healing us and rejuvenating us, body and soul. When we take the time to connect with them, to care for them, we can feel their energy and their power. We can feel their connection to the earth and the world around us. We can feel their connection to the cycle of life. When we use their medicines, we are tapping into this power, this connection. We are tapping into something that is both ancient and sacred.

Throughout the weekend, we participated in different workshops and activities that helped us to connect with ourselves and the abundant nature around us. We learned about different meditation techniques, how to connect with our intuition, and how to create and formulate a nature-based skincare routine.

One of the most memorable moments of the retreat was when we went on a night walk through the forest. We left our phones and flashlights behind and let the moonlight guide our way. This was a powerful exercise in trust and letting go. I felt like I was truly able to surrender and be held by Mother Nature for the first time in longer than I could remember.

The moon has long been associated with mysticism and magic. In many cultures, it is seen as a symbol of feminine energy, and its cycle of waxing and waning is often likened to the ebb and flow of life itself.

On this night, the moon was almost full and bright, casting a silver light over the rugged landscape. As we hiked along the narrow paths of the North Yorkshire moors, its cool dark energy fueled us. We felt alive and connected to something greater than ourselves. The moon is a powerful reminder that we are part of something larger than our day-to-day lives. It is a source of strength and inspiration, and its light guides us on our journey through life.

Just as the moon waxes and wanes, so too do our emotions and energy levels. Just as the seasons change in a never-ending dance, the tide ebbs and flows with the pull of the moon, and even our own body's cycles are governed by the rotation of the lunar cycle. Each phase of the moon corresponds with a different phase in our own lives. The new moon is a time for new beginnings when we can set our intentions for the month ahead. As the moon grows fuller, our energy levels rise, and we feel more creative and confident. The full moon is a time of culmination when our intentions and hard work come to fruition. Finally, as the moon wanes and grows dark, we experience a time of release and letting go. In nature, everything is in a state of constant flux, and we are no exception. By attuning ourselves to the lunar cycle, we can flow with nature's rhythms and lead more balanced, harmonious lives.

When the weekend came to an end, I didn't want to leave. I felt like I had finally started to come home to myself. I knew that I needed to find ways to keep this connection alive when I returned to my busy life.

It was as if something inside of me had been awakened. I could feel a stirring, a deep longing to return to my roots. I wasn't sure what it meant, but I knew I had to follow the call. And so, I began to remember. I remembered the healing modalities that had been passed down to me, the ones that had been so deeply buried as I tried to hold down a "proper job." I remembered the joy that I had once felt in practicing them. And slowly, tentatively, I began to unfurl. To allow myself to once again be open to the possibility of healing. It was a process that was both gentle and powerful, one that led me back to my true nature. Back to the place where I belonged.

As I allowed myself to remember and heal, I also began to share my knowledge with others. I found that there were many people who were searching for the same thing I was. They were looking for a way to connect with their own healing power, and they were looking for guidance on how to do that. I was happy to be able to share what I had learned, and I soon found myself teaching more and more. It was a natural evolution of my own healing journey, and it is something that brings me great joy.

Today, I am proud to say that I am a healer, or rather that healing for others moves through me. I am a channel for healing. I have reconnected with my roots, and I am able to share the gifts that I have been given with others. I am grateful for the path that has led me here, and I am excited to see where it takes me next.

Since attending the retreat, I have made it a priority to connect with nature on a daily basis. I go for walks in the park, meditate in my garden, spend time barefoot in the grass, and make my own natural body and skincare products.

This was just the beginning of my rewilding journey. A journey to remember my soul's purpose and how to keep her replenished and connected to nature in a world that can so easily make us forget. We are powered by nature. We are part of nature.

Soul rejuvenation is so important because it allows us to connect with ourselves on a deeper level. It helps us to remember who we are and what we're here to do. When we make time for this kind of soul care, we can let go of the stress and anxiety that come from living a life that's out of alignment with our true nature.

If you're feeling lost, disconnected, and searching for more meaning in your life, I invite you to begin your own journey of soul rejuvenation. This is when we take time to connect with our true nature — the part of us that is connected to the earth and all of its wisdom. Reconnect with nature and remember who you really are. It just might change your life.

I'm so grateful that I took the action I needed to break the pattern of lack of self-care and feeling powerless in my own life and attended the nature retreat. It was a powerful experience that helped me to remember what's important in life. Now, I make sure to rejuvenate every day, even if it's just for a few minutes. I take a walk in nature, meditate, or do some yoga, usually still in my pajamas, because life's about letting things be easy when they can be. More pleasure and play. Less pushing and striving. Soul rejuvenation has become an essential part of my life and I hope it can be part of yours too.

A weekend getaway turned into a life-changing experience that led me back to myself and my connection with nature. If you're looking for a soul-rejuvenating experience, I highly recommend retreating to nature in whichever way you can. A few minutes each day to notice the flower petals and leaves of your garden plants or the morning birdsong on your daily commute can make a huge difference. It just might be the best decision you ever make.

About Jo Capel

Jo is an entrepreneur and community builder. She is passionate about helping leaders build communities that create positive impact and do good in the world.

She loves discovering the unique dynamics that make each one thrive. After studying and working with community leaders all over the world, she founded her own company to help them build profitable communities with purpose.

She is passionate about her work and believes wholeheart-edly in the power of community to change lives for the better. Jo is the founder of the world's largest community exclusively for solo women vanlife enthusiasts, Women's Vanlife Collective.

Jo is also a holistic healing practitioner and teacher specializing in mycology and the restorative nature of plants and medicinal mushrooms. She is an angelic Reiki master, aromatherapist, and herbalist.

Currently living in West Yorkshire, Jo enjoys exploring in her campervan, wild food foraging, and visiting sacred sites across the U.K.

www.womensvanlifecollective.com

Do You Think the Stars Are Jealous of The Moon?

The wounds of the sacred feminine will have you stay in places you don't belong.

Being in the company of people who make you weak, not strong.

It is the thing that has you in a perpetual state of suffering and longing for a love that was never meant to be.

Because your sacred feminine lives from the heart and not just by what she sees.

But my sweet sister, beautiful sacred soul, the moon is cyclical in nature, and at times, some things must go.

Have you ever wondered why life turned out as it has? Have you explored deeply the wounding and wanderings that inform your daily existence? Have you questioned the things you have allowed both historically and presently in the name of love? I do not speak of love in just the romantic sense. I speak of love from your parents, your siblings, your culture, your friends, and society as a whole. Where in life have you stifled your own growth to pacify the masses? The story that informs those decisions wants to be explored, so it can unfurl and reveal to you all that is ready to be seen. That fear of persecution, do you even know where it begins? The too muchness that stops you from taking up "too much" space. That part of you that hesitates even when an invitation is made. What happens when the lights are turned all the way up? When fullness and radiance are naturally embodied in a transcendent state?

Historically, I know these outcomes have left a mark. A wounded, battered and deeply bruised heart. Yet somehow you, you manage to live as love. Holding with such reverence the truth of love and its light in every face you see. Those who have sought to lessen you know not the glory of the moon. They do not understand that tides have changed, and lives evolved with each phase. Whether full, waxing, waning, or appearing absent in the dark. A light such as you sends ripples out into every heart.

So, you are afraid to shine your light? I can understand this to a certain extent. To have been continuously told that you are too much would have anyone questioning the validity of their light. The light you exude lights up even the darkest night of any soul. You are the radiance of the moon in all her phases. Do you not realize your light is as essential as great Mother Moon? For the tides of life are moved by the presence of you too. I know, I know life has gifted you lessons time and again. Where being your most radiant self felt like waving a red rag at a bull. Their already wounded state wanting to lay to waste what you have so painstakingly built. Those who are so crippled by fear, seeing your forward movement as a direct challenge to their way of life. And I guess, in all honesty, in some ways, it is exactly that. Your radiance is a call to action for all those that are readying to take their first tentative steps into sovereignty, into integrity, into a deep-rooted dignity. This call awakens those who slumber, it will stir something deep that knows there is more that awaits. But those who feign sleeping states will demand you not disturb them in their work to put to bed those who dare to shine too bright. Sweet soul, shine anyway. No matter the offense they take. Do you think the stars are jealous of the moon?

Just as the fullness of the moon calls for release of anything not aligned to sacred truths, so too will your most radiant, beautiful, fully lit self feel like an invitation. It says … come … come with me, let's light up even the darkest night with our combined shine, so that none are left stumbling around as if completely blind. I know being turned all the way up can feel like a danger you have faced one too many times. Those meant to keep you safe, made the diminishing of you, a mission in their life. But, sweet soul, know this: it is a reflection of themselves. You have not driven them to distraction. They are in their own private hell. Unsupportive of themselves, so cannot support you by deed, or word, or action. No star has ever been jealous of the moon. For each knows that together they illuminate any space they occupy.

Do not let anyone feel comfortable with asking you to dim yourself. No friend, no foe, no kith nor kin has the right to deprive the world of the wonder that is you. Sacred moon personified, know that you are as ancient as time itself. You have been lighting up Universes within Universes since the creator dreamed of you and you were eventually inevitably birthed. Upon your arrival sending out ripples that moved the Heavens and the Earth. Your light has changed landscapes of mind, bodies and souls. So, brighten up the world around you as only you truly can. Let none lead you astray. For some are meant to light up the night sky and others light it up by day. The Sun and the Moon do not compete for the affections of the skies. They each understand that they have a rightful place that no one else can occupy. Do not let another tell you your rightful place. You will know it by the way it echoes in your heart and see yourself upon its face.

I encourage you to seek surroundings, people and places that see you in your sacred truth. Ones that feel blessed in your presence for they too shine brightly for any and everyone to see. They ask of you to just be who and what you truly came to be. You are the radiance of a full illumined moon, my love — do not just twinkle like you are a star.

Sweet soul, I know it is not always easy to follow the example of great Mother Moon. The moon, she is a wild one and calls all to be free, she shines her light on all things, including you and me. But first, you are called to surrender and trust the truth that is resident in your sacred beating heart. That you, beloved, are an example of the creator and love made into living art. Yours is a light meant to ignite hearts, minds, bodies, and souls. To reach far and wide, across all lands. Transcending the veil of illusion that creates separation, abandonment, and judgment, of self or at another's hands. No more does betrayal or denial of self require you to move against your natural ebb and flow. The more you surrender, the more you seem to illuminate and then emanate that otherworldly glow. You are a piece of magic that affects the tides within and without. You are a beacon, a miracle, a holy place — of this, there is no doubt. Awaken fully to who you are, allow this to fully land. Know that the love of the Divine works through you and always guides your hand.

So, remember today, tomorrow, and forever more. No star was ever jealous of the moon. You are free to be who and what you are and do what you came to do ... SHINE.

About Babita Gill

My name is Babita Gill and I live in beautiful Bournemouth, England. I am an ordinary woman moving through life experiencing some extraordinary things. For the past 22 years I have had the great privilege of working with men, women and children of all ages and stages of life. Supporting them using therapeutic techniques to explore the human condition, so they might understand themselves more deeply.

Over the last 10 years, I have also worked as a transformational alchemist, working as a multidimensional healer, writer, painter, photographer, and sculptor. My work has gifted me the opportunity to work with clients internationally. Nothing brings me deeper joy than when I am able to walk besides someone as they move through the journey of metamorphosis. Seeing them living and loving to their fullest and highest potential is always truly a humbling and awe-inspiring experience.

If you would like to know more about the work I do, please do come say hello on my Instagram page, @babita_gill. I would love to hear from you.

Epiphany on Platform 3

Had I known it was going to happen that day I might have planned a slightly grander, more inspiring location for the scene to unfold. Maybe I'd have been splashing around beneath a magical waterfall somewhere exotic, or musing dreamily on an expansive, white, sandy beach, listening to the gentle, lapping waves, admiring the endless, multi-colored sunset, or frolicking in a spring flower-filled meadow, maybe with some little lambs thrown in for good measure.

I probably wouldn't have chosen platform 3 at Slough station.

Nevertheless, that was indeed where it happened.

"It" being what I can only describe as a moment of extreme existential clarity, a soul awakening. A flash of "fuck yes" that would change the course of my life forever. Once I'd exited Slough station, anyway. I must say I'm not entirely sure what I was even doing in Slough station at the time.

What I DO know and what I DID know at the time was what I would do next.

But before we move on, we must journey back a little for some context on what I was seeking clarity for in the first place.

Back to around four months earlier.

I'd been working in media and advertising in London for the last fuckteen years and as I had climbed my way up the ranks, I had also become painfully aware of my soul slowly, but surely, dying. My once exciting, powerful, promising media career had become really quite empty and meaningless. Call me mad but spending year after year dreaming up ever more manipulative ways to entice people to buy some shitty shower gel just really wasn't lighting my heart on fire anymore. The long hours, noisy open plan offices, endless drunken nights out and intolerable office banter was destroying me quietly from the inside out. Not to mention the incessant pitching and performing and presenting and so many people.

And by people I of course mean people to please. What other kind were there?

Clients to please. Managers to please. Other team members to please. Directors to please. Suppliers to please. Luckily, I was indeed very, very good at pleasing all the people having spent a lifetime practicing and had been suitably rewarded with director status. Not rewarded with board-level status though, obviously. That appeared to be reserved for people who ignored instructions and did what they liked ... whereas I was also very good at doing what I was told. Including staying in my lane. And in my box. And therefore, in my good girl's director position.

And there I stayed. Until, after being signed off sick with yet another unpronounceable autoimmune issue and burnout, I realized that I had to get out.

So, I did the thing any lost, helpless, downtrodden soul with no idea what she wanted or who she even was any more would do, and I took a job somewhere even worse.

I was flattered into it.

I was head-hunted. They told me I was brilliant. Amazing. That I'd love it, that they loved me.

They offered me head-swelling amounts of money and some kind of gym membership.

And it was my ticket out.

And I'd forgotten how to say no. So, I did what I did best and said yes.

Had I listened to every cell in my body yelling, "DON'T YOU FUCKING DARE, WE'RE DOOOOOOMED," instead of deciding it was just nerves and the voice of inadequacy talking, I could have saved myself the next three months of actual hell.

But I didn't, and off to hell I trotted, in my smart new suit (I hate suits). Because somebody else said I should.

Well, no prizes for guessing that it didn't go too well.

I did not fit in there. At. All.

I had no idea what anyone was talking about for most of the time.

Their work ethic was beyond toxic. The atmosphere was so oppressive. I could feel every last glimmer of the feminine I still had left from my lifetime in media just seeping out of my pores on a minute-by-minute basis. I was also entirely unqualified for the role and felt ridiculously stupid. Every. Single. Day.

(And I would just like to add that I am actually far from stupid — I have always been a straight-A kinda girl with a degree from Cambridge ... but this place made me feel incredibly stupid. And pathetic. And anyway, everyone else there had posher sounding Cambridge degrees than mine so mine didn't count.)

I sat in meetings and said nothing. Even when it was my turn to speak, I opened and closed my mouth like an inane goldfish in complete paralysis. Mind blank. Body numb. Palms sweaty. Willing it to end.

I fantasized about exotic illnesses I might be able to come down with. Daydreamed about accidentally falling in front of a bus. Or of winning the lottery so I could run away and never go back.

(I did that once. I worked in a hairdressers for one morning. It felt exactly the same in my body as this place. I escaped out the back door when nobody was looking and ran home crying to my mum. She phoned and said my period had started so I couldn't come back … I didn't think the same approach would work this time, sadly.)

I worked all night on one occasion. They'd given me a project with a ridiculous turnaround, a flimsy brief, no guidance, and no background on the client. So, I stayed up all night to do it. They didn't use my work. Not a single bit. Nor did I get any feedback. They were nice like that.

I felt so trapped and helpless, and I hated every second of it.

And then I had my three-month review.

And for the first time in my life, I failed. I fucking failed!

I didn't pass my probation. I was being chucked out. That very day. I was allowed to go back to the office to collect my things and then, please politely fuck off.

I should have been overjoyed to be free at last. Instead, I was devastated, heartbroken, bereft, and absolutely terrified.

How was I such a shit person that I was being thrown out of a job? How was I so awful that every single person they'd asked for feedback had berated me? ME!? But I'm a good girl and I please people and people must love and praise me. How has this happened!?

And also, how was I supposed to live now without a job!?

Despite this new persona of mine I'd been trying to cultivate to fit into this hideous hell hole of a place being so unbearably uncomfortable, without it I had no idea who I was supposed to be or what I was supposed to do.

So, I cried. A lot. I swore a bit too. But mostly I cried.

I think they call it an ego death ... by the way, if you're going to have one, I can highly recommend doing it as you walk around an overcrowded Winter Wonderland on Thanksgiving with a blind-drunk husband — it adds a certain *je ne sais quoi* to the energy of the whole thing.

So, there I sat, newly unemployed and without my head-swelling London director's salary, at home in my rancid old pajamas staring at the wall wondering who I was and what I was going to do.

And for the next few weeks I played a torturous game with myself of obsessing over all the job vacancies in the London media agencies I'd been so desperate to escape a few months earlier.

Except now I felt even more downtrodden and invisible than I did before, and I wasn't convinced I'd even be able to get any of them. Instead of getting excited when I read the job specs, my heart sank a little further with every one. I found a few I knew I could do, and a few others I'd probably be able to do if I could just find my confidence under this pile of shame and confusion that had built up on top of it. I made a list of all the ones I would apply for.

And then continued to stare at the wall in a state of utter confusion and bewilderment. It felt as if somebody had taken my entire life, my entire personality and ripped it all up into shreds, jumbled it all up, shaken it about, and then shoved it back together again. And now I was left trying to disentangle and unravel and unpick the whole sorry mess to make some kind of a semblance of a life out of it.

And then, for some reason, I got on a train to Slough and spent the entire journey (for transparency, that's only seven minutes, so sounds a lot more dramatic than it was) nearly giving myself a hernia trying to make sense of the tangled-up web of despair in my mind.

And then, as I stepped off the train and onto platform 3, into a beautiful shaft of sunlight that had appeared from somewhere, it hit me.

Not the train, thankfully, but the truth.

And it came in the form of these words ... "Just because I COULD do it, doesn't mean I SHOULD do it. Just because I CAN do it, doesn't mean I want to. Or that I have to. Or that I'm going to."

COULD I get another job in media? ... Abso-fucking-lutely! Did I WANT to? About as much as poking myself in the eye with a sharp stick.

So, was I going to? NO, I WAS NOT!

Would everybody else think I was insane? Yes. Would it be totally irresponsible to throw away the chance of that kind of a salary with a mortgage and bills to pay? Probably. Would I be any good at another job in media? Absolutely.

But was I willing to continue to live somebody else's life? To do what somebody else told me to do, how they told me to do it? To wait until somebody else noticed I might be worthy of a promotion? To sacrifice my soul in the pursuit of position and money? To do what other people expected? To play all the mind games to get ahead? To squash and mold myself to fit in? To put my body's needs, my heart's desires second to my "career?" To do something, day in, day out, that I had no passion for, no interest in and that didn't light me up one little bit?

No. I was not.

And so, in that moment, on platform 3 at Slough station I made a vow. To follow my heart. To stop squashing myself. To stop willingly climbing into the boxes and jumping through the hoops other people had laid out for me. To stop saying "yes" because I thought that was the answer they wanted to hear and instead say "yes" to myself. And to only ever do things that I wanted to do and in ways I wanted to do them.

I took a picture of the platform exactly where it happened to capture the moment.

And then I retrained as a teacher.

And I became a mother.

And I learned a whole shit-ton more about people-pleasing and playing the good girl and comparisonitis.

And I built a business helping other mothers fuck all of that off to become the true, whole, authentic, unapologetic, fully alive women they're here to become.

And I couldn't be happier.

And truthfully, I wouldn't change the Slough station part. Because the wonderful thing is that these moments are everywhere. The magic is in the everyday. We can spend a lifetime searching for the grand gestures and the breathtaking moments only to miss all those fantastic little bits and all the juicy lessons they hold for us along the way. Real life happens at places like Slough station, so it was the perfect place to start the second half of mine.

About Emma While

Emma While is a mother, an early-years and adult learning specialist, positive psychology geek, lover of squirrels, wild swimmer, NLP practitioner, mindfulness teacher, writer, and owner of Courage & Chamomile (purveyors of transformational coaching for mums since 2016).

Since breaking free from her own suffocating little cage (of society's expectations of her as well as those she had foisted upon herself), Emma has been passionate about empowering other mums to do the same ...

... to believe in and become their FULL and unapologetic selves, beyond the identity of "mum" or any other roles they play. To let go of the shame, the guilt, the rules, the "should" and the "should nots," the "I can'ts" and "I have tos." To break the cycles and the patterns, to consciously curate the passionate, exciting, and fulfilling life they both desire and deserve, and dream into being a future fit for the next generation we're raising ...

Not one where everybody just trudges along in the same old same old, doing as they're told ... but one where our children get to be their own independent thinkers, makers and leaders ready to carve out their own unique paths in this world ... having watched us do it first.

Because right now, this world needs a change, and Emma believes that fully empowered, impassioned mothers are the ones to lead it.

www.instagram.com/courageandchamomile

Shine On, You Crazy Diamond

"Remember when you were young?
You shone like the sun
Shine on, you crazy diamond."
Credit — Pink Floyd

This song always sends shivers down my spine.

It always points me back to that part of me that was so lost for a long while.

The grown-up version of myself, the one who was desperately searching for love in all the wrong places. The one who never allowed herself to feel anything, numbing pain and emotion through throwing herself into work, drinking all the booze with a side of self-deprecating humor for good measure.

I remember when I started working in my first ever serious communications job. I was 19 at the time and had the world at my feet. I was bubbly, I was playful, I worked hard and was, according to my boss at the time, "a ray of sunshine."

I remember it well — this comment came from someone who was my dad's age with his own kids — so it was meant in the purest possible way.

In fact, it's written in my leaving card which is gathering dust along with all the other memories from that time. My last pair of pointe shoes. The key to the door from my 18th birthday card. Every leaving card from every job I received one from. Ticket stubs to my first Blur gig. Photographs of me at my first rave up — sporting heather shimmer lipstick and wearing Exclamation perfume. Memories of holiday romances and so many firsts.

I look back at those pictures of her — she who believed being rich was about how much money you made, things that you possessed, and finding the handsome prince to whisk you away.

That girl loved the romance. The idea of romance.

I wanted to be Lucky Santangelo from the Jackie Collins books I devoured over and over again. I loved the idea of strutting about with a briefcase and being in control. The idea of being a strong woman in a man's world.

Before that, I was only concerned with dancing. Being on stage fluttering around "being" a swan in our ballet school's version of *Swan Lake,* pretending to be an angry villager in the pantomime, or just feeling my body moving with ease and grace to the music.

At school, I went under the radar. I was vanilla, average even.

But on stage I allowed myself to shine. We shone.

There were five of us who danced together often, all the same age and level. Our teacher created group dances, and each of us was able to play to our strengths. Mine was the ability to jump higher than most — so I would be given the opportunity to leap across the stage. My friends were taller and super strong, so they were holding amazing poses with their legs going on forever.

On stage performing together was the one place I never felt in competition with the others.

We showed up, did our best, supported each other, practiced together, we worked towards a common goal.

We danced together, effortlessly and with grace.

Of course, off stage was a different matter. Mainly because our dance teacher felt the need to pit us against each other to get the best out of us. Or when we were sat at the end of the day, waiting to see who had won the gold medal in the category we had performed our solo dances in.

I hated that part, all gazing round at each other sitting at the edge of our seats, hoping it was us winning this time, but then feeling the mix of happiness for your fellow dancer and the green-eyed monster lurking just in the wings.

Funny that competition came into it at all, really — because in the group dances, we needed to trust and support each other to be in perfect alignment. In fact, I am quite surprised I am writing about that time at all.

But it was a time when, for the most part, my body and I were happy.

It was a time when I did shine like a crazy diamond.

Yes, it was hard work, but I loved it — the stage make-up, the uncomfortable fishnet tights, and the sparkling beautiful costumes my mum would spend hours creating. The euphoria of taking a bow to applause knowing you just nailed that routine you had been practicing in your sleep.

Nothing flipping better.

So back to Lucky and her power-dressing. I decided to knuckle down and get my GCSEs — my dance teacher wouldn't allow me to take time off to study for my exams, and then return to my dancing — which had been my proposal to her and my mum. Mum was happy to support me in whatever. My dance teacher, on the other hand, shut me down and said if I was serious about dancing, I would be able to do both.

I didn't feel I could. The fact I was excelling in dancing — my shelves were littered with trophies, medals, and programs of the shows I had starred in — didn't seem to matter to her.

Though I wonder now if she put pressure on me because she saw something I didn't.

That I had potential to succeed as a dancer, and whilst schoolwork is important, following my dreams may have been more important. It just wasn't communicated in that way.

It was a flat no, no explanation or compromise.

That was that.

So, there we have its decision made.

My life of dancing was over; I had been dancing since I was seven.

I remember I was told in passing that I could have applied for the Ballet Rambert, but I never felt the comment was meant for me. It wasn't a clear directive. It was a throwaway mention that I never followed up on. A fantasy — because that was what it was, wasn't it? A dream.

I mean, who made a career out of living your dream?

Life was about doing the right thing. Following the clear education path laid out in front of me — getting an adequate education. Attending school, then college ... and after that, deciding if university was next or going out to work.

I remember being asked by a coach of mine to do an exercise around all the times I felt I had dimmed to fit in.

This moment was one of those. Whether me deciding to be sensible and focus on my exams was when I felt I needed to dim to fit in, or me accepting that ultimatum from my dance teacher was another.

I am sure we have had moments like these in life where we felt we were doing the right thing.

I often wonder what would have happened if I had followed the dancing path? I know friends who did, and they became dancers on cruise ships and in the chorus on the West End.

I sometimes put my pointe shoes on just to reconnect with her. The girl who danced.

Would I have been happy in that life, I wonder?

After my college exams — it became about the quest.

The quest to find the handsome prince, the job that would enable me to get the fast car and the briefcase. I kissed a lot, A LOT of frogs.

In fact, I wish someone had told me that the best way to get the guy is to not chase, to not throw yourself at their mercy or perform whatever weirdness they asked of you.

There where multiple times I gave my power away, drunken gropes with strangers, one-night stands, I cringe when I think of the danger I put myself in at times.

Somehow, though, I found my way. In fact, I settled a lot along the way. I took the first job I could find as a medical secretary because I was out of inspiration. With dancing no longer in my life, I coasted along rudderless. Then came the nudges. A nurse I worked with suggested I investigate publicity.

It felt significant. It felt like purpose calling.

I promptly left my job to go work in sales (the closest thing to publicity that I could find). Then at the last moment, I felt the twang of my body telling me it wasn't right. So, jobless, I signed up to a temp agency.

And walked right into a job in a publicity and communications department.

One thing I've noticed about the 23 years I have been in communications and publicity, is so very often you become the supporting act.

You are the person behind the scenes making sure the main event is showing up and shining.

You are the one ensuring all the dots are aligned. The fixer. The only person who knew how to work the overhead project and laptop together. If you have ever watched *The Devil Wears Prada*, the scene where the main character is stood behind Meryl Streep's character, explaining who each of the guests are and doing the necessary intros, sums it up aptly.

For years I skulked in the background in my little black number, or my white shirt and trousers combo; I was even mistaken as a waitress at one event — true story.

I sound like this was a problem for me — it really wasn't.

For many years I was very comfortable playing the supporting role. Remember the vanilla version of Sarah at school. She was running the show, though, this time.

From time to time, Dreamer Sarah popped up. That creative part of me started to rear its head, and I began to have big ideas. And I was given the opportunity to share those ideas; but, typically, I would share my ideas, and then they would be claimed by others — it was infuriating.

Only when I pushed hard for promotion, spoke up in meetings and ensured I was supporting my boss, who had the ear of the C-level, did I then get the opportunity to co-lead a huge global project, did I get that chance to shine. It was the 25th anniversary of the company I worked for, and my colleague and I suggested a 25-hour round-the-world party — which involved the passing of a virtual time capsule. It was a huge event which kicked off in the US, with each country holding an event which followed the sun around the world. It was an epic amount of work, but wow, it was amazing to witness.

And guess what — at the end of the day, when the 25 hours were done? The leadership patted themselves on the back for a job well done.

Another lesson I have learned.

To accept that my ideas are not always mine — in fact, I do not own them. I think Liz Gilbert explains this well in her book *Big Magic*. She talks about having a creative idea around a book, and then because she doesn't act on it at the time, someone else picks up that idea and runs with it. I see it all the time in the entrepreneurial industry. I feel like there is a big download shared with many of us at the same time, and it is open to our own interpretation. So, we go ahead and execute the idea, and then find someone else is doing something so very similar — it's not ours to own — it's ours to pull and use that inspiration as we feel best suits. I digress.

Again, looking back on that time, I realize that opportunity came after I had put in the graft. When I understood the company and the product I was promoting. And when I had fully allowed Dancer Sarah to be present in the creation of the event, that's when the magic started to shine through.

It was only then was I ready to really step up and shine.

The same can be said with my own journey as an entrepreneur, a human walking this earth, and a mother to my children.

When I danced out of corporate life nearly five years ago, it took a little while to find my feet, my voice, and get clarity on who I wanted to serve.

And who I wanted to run the show. The shiny crazy diamond or the vanilla version.

When I figured out what I wanted and how I wanted to show up and shine in the world, it was like I had been given the keys to the kingdom again.

I could almost hear the bolts unlocking.

One thing is for sure — Dancer Sarah is no longer sitting in the memory box.

She is front and center in her own life, on her own stage, and dances alongside her clients, sisters, and friends. It is possible to get back to the best version of you — you just need to be brave enough to make that choice every single day.

I invite you to dance with me. We are all diamonds. Multi-faceted and unique in our own way.

Shine on, you crazy diamond.

About Sarah Lloyd — PR Alchemist, Radio Presenter, and Author

In the media and PR business for 25 years, Sarah Lloyd quit her global corporate PR leadership role in 2017, in a bid to be a master of her own and to bring a better balance to her life, leading her to create a more magical approach to publicity. An intuitive, angel communicator, and Reiki energy master herself, she specializes in working in "flow," so has thrown the PR rule book out the window.

Her mission is to teach and guide others to share their stories, without fear, on their terms. Specializing in her own brand of magic-based, conscious PR and communications, her Alchemy strategy sessions help to ignite the fire within, acknowledge blocks, and help to transmute all that has held clients back from stepping up and sharing their mission and purpose.

In March 2020 she published her book, *Connecting the Dots — A Guide to Making Magic with the Media*, via The Unbound Press.

www.indigosoulpr.com

Out of The Shadows...
Into the Light

Like many little girls growing up in the 70s and 80s, I spent my summers wearing cheesecloth and legwarmers, singing ABBA songs, recording myself on a cassette deck, and ripping my skirt off along with Bucks Fizz. I wanted to perform and shine and to be seen in my sweet, glowing, girly charm.

As I grew older, being seen as special or shining became less and less safe. When I moved to secondary school, fighting at lunchtime was very common. It was a good idea to play small and not be visible if you wanted to avoid trouble — the limelight was not a wise place to be if you wanted a safe, quiet life.

So, I took refuge in books, visiting the library as often as I could. I devoured shelves of history, literature, and biography. Then, inevitably, my burgeoning sexuality started to blossom. I was fascinated by sex at a young age. My secret pleasure was to race to the well-thumbed "naughty bits" of the bestsellers of the day and melt into the scenes. I still remember the winds of *Mistral's Daughter*, the penthouses of *Hotel*, and the tight jodhpurs of *Riders*. I was fascinated by the desire, the seduction, the yet unknown pleasures.

But soon I learned that my emerging woman's body wasn't safe.

On a walk down a quiet local footpath in the afternoon, I was pushed to the ground by two older boys who pulled at my clothes.

I was one of the lucky ones. My screams pierced the afternoon sky, and the boys ran off.

I ran to a local playground and confided in a girlfriend I knew from my school. She was fairly sympathetic, but in the coming days she and another girl used the information to humiliate me. It left a lasting distrust in female friendship.

Then there was my Catholic upbringing. The teachings of the Church reminded me constantly about the sins of the body and the ignominy of the teenage mother. I went to Mass every day for a while, prayed with my rosary and begged the Lord to forgive me my sins — even though I had no idea what they were. I was indoctrinated. My natural curiosity and enjoyment of the body was something shameful and wrong.

All of this was set against the rising backdrop of panic about AIDS. TV and magazine adverts portrayed icebergs of fear that loomed over us all. Sex equals death — or at least that's what I took it to mean.

By the time I reached university, aged 18, I wore men's jumpers and baggy jeans. I drank pints of beer with the boys. By joining their ranks, I could hide in plain sight. I was safe.

But underneath these layers of protection was a beautiful, sexual young woman, full of passion and desire. It's hard to write that even now. Who am I to claim my own sexuality, to declare myself beautiful? How arrogant! How vain!

Like many of us, I had nowhere safe to express my sexuality, no place to be seen as an adult sexual being. My sexual self was only allowed to peek out in nightclubs at 1:45 am, before the lights went on, taking that final walk around the dancefloor to see if I could find someone to kiss and remind myself that I really exist.

Entering the world of corporate work, as a marketing professional in publishing, I wore the uniform grey Next suit. I ensured that my skirts were long enough — in fact, trousers were my best friend. My necklines were demure. I tried hard to never seduce or be seduced by a boss or colleague.

Be a good girl, don't step out of line, don't cause any trouble.

But after too many drinks, the lustful woman was hard to keep in check.

Like many around me, as my 30s came along, I settled into a partnership, bought a house, planned for marriage and children. Then came a shattering relationship breakup that left me bereft and alone (but that's another story).

Before long I was viscerally missing physical touch and sex. I wondered if paying for sex was the answer. I daydreamed about visiting hotel lobbies and seducing the traveling salesmen.

My sensual, sexual, soulful woman was aching to be set free — but I was a caged bird.

By the age of 40, life had become stale and dull. Work felt like a chore. I was single and childless. Online dating was an endless series of disappointments.

I knew I wanted more ... and I had no idea how to find it.

It's 2007. I'm living in Menlo Park, California, working in another corporate job. One day I wandered into the East/West bookstore. There was a meditation class about to begin. I stepped into that class and into a new life. I discovered spirituality and Reiki and clary sage. It was an awakening for my soul, but I felt a vast chasm between the day-to-day mundanity of my life and the expansion I was touching into through meditation and avidly reading the great spiritual teachers.

Then, one day as I was traveling for work, I read an article in an in-flight magazine about a personal development holiday in Spain at a retreat center called Cortijo Romero. On a whim (or was it something higher?), I booked. I wish I had kept the article, as it was the catalyst to a new life. On that holiday I danced, did sun salutations in the mountain air, swam at night and slept under orange trees. I read Deepak Chopra and sang mantras. It was as if my soul had found a place to emerge from dull, grey corridors into bright lemony sunlight. I had found personal development!

My next step was a New Year workshop with Jan Day. It was titled "Passion, Power and Love." I guess I was drawn to these three qualities I was longing to embody in my life. I had no idea that Jan's other work was based around Tantra. I remember a fellow participant on the first day asking me if I had done Tantra before. My response was "Tantra, who the f**k said anything about Tantra?"

One of the first exercises involved standing in the center of a small group, choosing whether to be touched by one, or two, or three people — or not at all. I had not experienced touch from another for years. It broke me open.

I had found a place to be fully seen. I could be messy and full of grief. Angry and resentful. Wild and passionate.

All of me. All of me. All of me.

The daily morning meditations gave me a space to explore all the lost parts of myself. I could be wild or shy, bold or soft. I could sound my fierce anger and howl my unfulfilled sexual woman.

I found a deeply, wildly feminine woman with undulating hips. A goddess who relishes pleasure. I got to meet a part of me who needed to beat the floor with my fists and scream the pain and hurt. I welcomed in the mother who had never had the chance to exist. I could now hold a friend in hurt and soothe their pain with a tender stroke and a calm presence.

I have a clear memory of standing in front of a mirror, smiling with the sight of my own magnificence that I had never seen before.

I claimed my own beauty.

I was touched by the love and presence and honoring of my fellow humans.

The layers of conditioning began to fall away.

I made new friendships of depth, commitment, and honesty.

I began to trust women for the first time.

I began to trust men.

I didn't change overnight. These layers of good girl conditioning run deep.

I felt ashamed sometimes — and I felt I was *being* shamed sometimes. Was I weird? A workshop junkie? A flake?

Even as I write this piece, the shame still creeps in. Who might be reading? My mum? My former business colleagues? What will they think? Will they judge me? Am I being too much?

And I know this shame is not mine. It belongs with religion, with patriarchy, with societal conditioning. My beautiful being is innocent.

Eventually my continued commitment to transformational work gave me the courage to change career and retrain as a sex and relationship therapist.

It took determination and sacrifice to find the money to retrain, but I am so proud of my transformation. My new vocation is a privilege and an honor. I speak daily with people about their most intimate lives. I run groups where sexuality is an open topic of discussion and where men and women are able to discover who they are and be honored and loved just as they are.

Now that I work in the field of sexuality, I frequently hear that attending a webinar or a group call is something that most people would find difficult, because this is such private territory. I understand this, and fiercely respect my clients' need for confidentiality and privacy, yet part of me aches that there is still so much shame and embarrassment about speaking publicly — or even privately — about our sexuality. This hiding ultimately leads to behavior being pushed into the shadows.

Many women I speak with only have experience of sex that feels like a duty or burden, something to be fitted in between childcare and chores. Some tell me that they are only really able to be sexual when drunk, becoming reckless in the grip of their own desire — which is usually kept well-hidden and rigidly controlled. And of course, so many sisters are still left with the ghosts of sexual abuse.

Now my work and passion is helping women, men, and couples to discover a more empowered relationship with their sexuality. Together we explode old myths, explore how to bust out of tired patterns, and shake off outdated, unhelpful beliefs. We befriend all the parts — the parts that are in touch with desire and wanting and the parts that work hard to protect and keep us safe. We uncover the unique sensual essence that has been pushed down.

I believe sexuality is a natural aspect of being human.

I see sexual energy as life force and a light that helps us shine.

Desire can put a spring in our step and a grin on our face.

Arousal can bring gifts of joy, laughter, and delight.

Pleasure is our goddess-given birthright.

Sexual energy is both powerful and innocent.

It brings me so much joy to work in the service of restoring more love and connection in the world. My soul sings to have found a way out of the shadows and into the light.

About Nicola Foster

Hi, I'm Nicola Foster, Relationship and Intimacy Coach.

I help women and men who have relationship struggles to develop skills, confidence, and knowledge on how to enjoy more empowered and more conscious intimate relationships.

My favorite aspect of my work is supporting new and long-term couples to discover how they can build or deepen intimacy and trust with each other. I teach the Wheel of Consent and the practices of mindfulness and slowing down sex. I'm passionate about intimacy because when we can connect with each other safely, we feel happier, more relaxed, and more able to cope with life's challenges and ups and downs.

I'm based in Somerset in the southwest of the U.K. near Glastonbury, where I live with my partner Jason. I love to indulge my passions for sea swimming, the outdoor pool, walking in the woods and deepening my meditation and yoga practices, and conscious movement and dance. And, if all that sounds a little bit worthy, you'll be glad to know that some of my other passions are on the more indulgent side. I love a fancy spa, Michelin-star food and posh cocktails served in really cold glasses! Find me on Instagram at @realrelatingwithnicola

Ego Satis: I Am Enough

The most painful message I carried with me from my childhood was that I was simultaneously too much and not enough. I was too bossy, too energetic, too loud, too emotional, too sensitive, too selfish. And I was also not thin enough, not pretty enough, not smart enough, not kind enough, not polite enough ... not good enough.

This message played out in a variety of ways in my life. I learned to compartmentalize my emotions, perform and achieve at a high level, and care for others even at my own expense. I became a people-pleaser, an overachiever, and a perfectionist.

As children, we lack the ability to understand the subtleties of what is happening around us. According to Piaget's theory of cognitive development, most children don't begin to grasp abstract thinking until roughly age 12. It's no wonder we carry these skewed and sometimes corrupted messages with us into adulthood.

After graduating from college with a B.A. in biology and Spanish, I believed I only had two feasible options: pursue a PhD in molecular biology or pivot and pursue an MD. I decided to pivot away from research and pursue an MD, despite having said throughout my life I didn't want to go into medicine.

In six short weeks I studied for and ranked in the 88th percentile on the MCAT. And in only three months, I jumped through hoops and compiled my medical school application, submitting it just before the season closed. My efforts were rewarded with an interview, and I was offered a position at the University of South Dakota Sanford School of Medicine.

After starting medical school, I felt like I didn't deserve to be there. "They only accepted me because my mother is an alumnus." Although my first eighteen months passed uneventfully, I couldn't shake the feeling I didn't belong.

Once I began clinical rotations during my second year, I felt woefully incompetent and unprepared. If I didn't know the answer to my attending physicians' questions, I chastised myself, "You should know this!" I made myself miserable by believing I should already know what I was doing despite being a student.

Halfway through my clinicals (marking the start of year three), I began to relax and allow myself to just be a medical student. My performance improved and I enjoyed the process of learning to care for patients much more. I ultimately fell in love with surgery, feeling as if time stopped when I was in the OR. Being able to solve some-one's problem in such a concrete, hands-on way was so satisfying.

Towards the end of my third year, I began shaping myself into the best surgical applicant I could be. It must have worked, because I ended up interviewing at twelve general surgery programs across the U.S. and matched at my second choice. That's when the COVID-19 pandemic hit.

In May of 2020, my father and I packed up my car and drove from South Dakota to California. Even though the pandemic certainly put a damper on things, I remained excited to train at a level one trauma center. Sadly, my enthusiasm didn't last long.

On day one of residency, I was thrown into the fire. My first week on the trauma floor, I worked more than 80 hours and barely had time to eat one or two meals a day. The sheer volume of complex patients under my care was overwhelming. I lost ten pounds that month.

My first weekend, I was left to care for a patient in the emergency room who had been stabbed multiple times and almost died from internal bleeding. My third week, I switched to night shifts and was responsible for a census of 80-100 surgical patients. My fourth week, I pronounced a patient's death. She was younger than me. I had rounded on her daily during my first two weeks, but her health worsened. The photo of her four-year-old daughter was still taped to the wall across from her bed, and her lifeless body clutched a Mickey Mouse doll.

I went back to my work room and sobbed for five minutes. My pager kept beeping: more patients needed me. I dried my eyes and continued caring for the other 80+ patients on my list until sign-out came at 7 a.m.

Soon all the cracks in the facade of my residency program began to show. Our attending physicians expected us to know what we were supposed to do without ever being told. When we fell short of mindreading, we were ruthlessly criticized. Amongst all five classes of residents, gossip and fear ran rampant. Our patient loads were enormous, supervision was lacking, and the level of hostility by some faculty and senior residents was profound.

It was a truly miserable place to work. To give you an idea of how bad it was (and still is), the national attrition rate for general surgery residency is about 20%. In this program, 40% of the class of 2021 did not graduate. Out of five residents, one was held back, and another was held back and then fired.

At the end of my second month, I landed in hot water after disagreeing with my senior resident's patient care plan. I contacted my attending physician to discuss the care plan, because I was concerned it was not in our patient's best interest. Despite knowing it may come back to bite me, I decided it was more important that my patient receive the best care possible. My attending agreed with the senior resident, and I let it go.

A month later, I was called into the program director's office without warning. I was reprimanded for bringing my patient concern to her instead of trusting the decision-making of my senior resident. She said I carried myself as a know-it-all and didn't respect the authority of my senior residents. Supposedly there were "other examples," but she refused to divulge them. She said it would be a long five years for me if I didn't change.

In her office, something shattered inside of me. The void of being too much and not enough felt as if it would swallow me whole. I was giving this program everything I had — all of my waking hours, my intellect, my health, my sanity, my compassion, and it still wasn't enough. Out of exhaustion and frustration, tears streamed down my face. She refused to let me leave her office until I had "composed" myself.

I knew in my bones I had to leave this program. I'd already seen what it was doing to my peers and had done to the senior residents. For a few days, I lived in a state of anguish and total disillusionment, feeling like I had been robbed of my joy for learning and living.

Then an almost imperceptible voice whispered, "Trust yourself." I started to think, what if I quit residency tomorrow? What if I quit medicine altogether? I turned my gaze inward for guidance instead of looking outside of me. I was tempted to quit medicine altogether, but I decided to explore a different specialty first. Immediately I began making plans to transition from surgery to psychiatry.

Early in November, my phone rang with a number from Rhode Island. The assistant program director at Brown wanted to offer me an interview for a second-year position at their psychiatry residency. I was stunned. Two days later I interviewed via Zoom, and a week later I received a contract.

In my last conversation with my grandfather before he died from COVID, I shared my exciting news. He was in such good spirits, bragging about his staff at the VA and making plans with me to get a "cuppo-ccino" when we saw each other next. Gramps told me how much he loved me and how proud of me he was.

While I was thrilled to start fresh in psychiatry at Brown in July, I dreaded finishing the next seven months at my surgery program. Every day I had to remind myself it would be worth it. On the morning of Sunday, June 20, 2021, I finished my last night shift. I enjoyed my last day in California with good friends from the emergency medicine program. Monday morning, I awoke before dawn and flew from the west coast to the east coast. My psychiatry orientation started the very next day.

Despite everyone's kindness and warmth at Brown, I struggled to feel like I belonged. Soon the flashbacks began. I would see staff in blue scrubs and surgical caps in the hospital, and my brain would mistakenly identify someone as one of my former colleagues. I closed my eyes, shook my head, and reminded myself those people were thousands of miles away.

In August, I started to dread waking up for work. With increasing frequency, I would sarcastically think, "Just shoot me." One day I imagined climbing into a bathtub and submerging myself until the water went over my head and I didn't come up for air. I made excuses not to attend social events, and I didn't bother exploring new restaurants, shops, or parks around me. Outside of work, I would eat, sleep, watch TV, and spend time with my new dog, Lola.

Recognizing it was time to seek help, I confided in my new program director. We decided it was best for me to take vacation and enroll in a partial hospital program. Those two weeks in the partial program were painful but transformative.

My therapist at the partial program asked if I had heard of the sunk cost fallacy. She proposed that perhaps I stayed in medicine because of all the time and money I had sunk into it. In truth, I'd had doubts about a career in medicine for years, but I feared what people would think if I quit and how I would manage the $200,000 I had in student loan debt.

Confronting many challenging questions led me to ask my mother about my childhood. She hesitantly decided it was time to share a series of family trauma and conflict we had never discussed. When she finished, it felt like a piece of my puzzle fit into place. It partially explained the context behind me coming to feel that I was too much and not enough.

At the end of September, I decided to resign from residency to begin rekindling my joy and healing my wounds. A massive weight was lifted off my shoulders. Unfortunately, my parents thought I was making a huge mistake and they began to panic.

My father told me he would not help me move and that I was "throwing away every privilege [I] have." He said to me, "I'm not sure how much your mother and I will be able to support you if you quit." My mother had family friends in medicine call me to tell me what a big mistake I was making. My parents questioned if my medication was making me manic.

Despite their concerns, I decided to keep going. I signed my letter of resignation, and two days later I bought a used shuttle bus with plans to convert it into an RV. I packed my things and moved to Norwich, Connecticut, to live with my boyfriend. To make ends meet, I began teaching an online MCAT preparation course to pre-med students.

My boyfriend and I argued a lot (and ultimately broke up), but I kept pushing forward. In December, I had my right forearm tattooed with a beautiful design that includes a line from my favorite meditation and the Latin words *Ego satis*: I am enough. I started painting again, and in February I decided to join a co-working space.

I found joy in meeting people in the business world and expanding my circle of local friends. I learned to build my own website and started a blog. My paintings are currently on display at an art studio and bar in Norwich, and I am about to launch my own consultancy.

I have also reconciled with my family. As I write this, I am in Sioux Falls, South Dakota, working alongside my father to convert my bus. He recently told me I was a blessing and a source of joy in his life. My mom told me they would love me no matter what direction I take. I cried tears of relief, finally feeling seen and heard.

Disillusionment can be one of the most painful experiences we face, but it heralds growth. If we are kind and honest with ourselves, we can begin to look at the messages we have carried with us from childhood and decide to let go of those which no longer serve us. I am beginning to learn that average is not a dirty word, perfectionism leads to a lifetime of discontentment, and even if I don't always *feel* like it, I really am enough.

About Jessica Simpkins

Dr. Jess has more hats than she can count, but among them she considers herself an artist, writer, and entrepreneur. She has a passion for learning and believes her calling is to spread more joy, love, and kindness. At the time she submitted this piece of writing, she was living in Spokane, Washington, with her dog Lola and her parents. Dr. Jess and her father have been hard at work converting a 17-passenger shuttle bus into an RV. When she's not working on her bus, she's creating artwork, writing, frequenting coffee shops, meeting new people, and exploring local sites. You can find Dr. Jess creating videos on TikTok, sharing photos on her Instagram, and providing written updates on her Facebook.Visit her website here at https://www.drjessicasimpkins.com/ to learn more about Dr. Jess, follow her journey, or send her a message.

Reclaimed

Early on in life it was evident that the world had an expectation of the role I should play. How I was supposed to act, how I was supposed to look, how I was supposed to talk, even breathe at times, it seemed. I accepted that role and played it well. My supporting role as a great wife and great mom. I stayed home, a loving mother attending to my wifely duties. Supporting my husband in all his endeavors. But to what detriment? What happens when the lead walks out on his role?

You find yourself crumpled in a heap on the shower floor barely able to breathe as you try to process the papers you just received that brought your "fairytale" to an end. What about our four children? What about the grandson on the way? The new phase of life we are entering? Was I not enough? Was I not pretty enough? Didn't I give you everything? Did I miss this part of the script?

Complete disbelief, as 27 years of my life seemingly slips down the drain. What do I do now? I don't have all the answers, yet. But I do know they lie within me, waiting to be reclaimed.

<u>reclaiMEd</u>

It is as if the one I loved so deeply is dead.

Yet, you still walk this earth with breath in your lungs.

I long for touch, caress, the passion of your embrace. Even to see your face.

The one I loved no longer exists, realizing it is not you that I miss.

The dream of what was, never will be; at least not for you and me.

I have given so very much of myself till nearly nothing remained, nothing but pain.

Merely a glimmer of who I once was. Beaten down by what was supposed to be love.

Twinkle, sparkle, a glint of light, returns to mine eyes.

Nights are not as long nor dark, returning the fire within my heart.

Days are beginning to fill with smiles, sunshine and promise of what's to come.

Allowing myself to feel again, knowing that love and joy first come from within.

I am doing this for me, in spite of you.

Now is the time to dream of what is to be, but also, what's already inside of me.

Sorrow has no power over me.

This power is mine.

The power to love.

The power to laugh.

The power to heal from my broken past.

The power to start again.

The power to be whole.

Brokenness has served its purpose; I am forever grateful.

Having continued awareness of its life lessons.

No longer does it consume me. I reclaim me!

I am reclaiMEd.

Hope~

About Hope Futrell

Hope, mother of four, grammy of two and dog mom of one, grew up in Michigan and relocated to North Carolina in 2009. She loves the big city/country vibe that Raleigh, North Carolina offers, getting dressed up and going out on the town to spending time in nature hiking, restoring and exploring. Journaling, doodling and expressing herself in creative ways has always been a part of her, but writing and publishing her poem is a new adventure for her. She is excited to be a part of this collaborative book. The encouragement and lifting up of others, especially women, in a world of comparison, is her passion. She wants to be a light to help others see their beauty is all their own and discover that their own inner validation is their true superpower.

Dimming

The light within
Shining as it spins
Touching all with grace
Staying strong in place

Blowing out and in
The wind, it dims
Pressing in the heart
Pulling out a part

Growing hot and strong
The desire to belong
Pushing out the knowing
Limiting the growing

Breathing deeply, the cool
Returning sweetly, the fool
Wondering where it has been
Ah, the light within
-H. Iden

Ah, my light ... when did it dim? It has taken most of my life to understand that this was even a question. However, after some life, some love, and some compassion I did finally see that, indeed, a light had dimmed inside of me. I must admit, I am still in debate with myself as to whether or not this is entirely avoidable. It isn't anything you "wish" upon another. We do not aspire to hardships and broken hearts. When we do go down and then emerge from these depths, we bring with us a deeper understanding of ourselves, intertwined with raw love for who we are at our core.

My parents divorced when I was six years old. It was not a nice divorce. There was an affair, new relationships, and a big bad custody battle. Being the big sister, of course I protected my brother, kept the "adult" matters away. I didn't want him to see the fights or the tears. But I saw them. Time moved on and life is life, but so many times I was made to feel less for simply loving both of my parents. Over time, things shake out, as they always do, but I had changed. Through these events, I believed it was my responsibility to make other people happy; to be the people-pleaser. I learned also somewhere in this time that I wasn't good enough. I cannot recall it being one specific event, but simply society, what was happening in my direct life, and how people responded to me. I was a larger girl in comparison to many, I worked a lot, and I danced a lot. Dance classes were my only release. I had friendships, but I always felt like somewhat of a loner.

Where boys were concerned, I always thought I simply wasn't good enough or pretty enough. I did have boyfriends, though. A few very nice guys, a couple I wish to forget, and even a few I wish I had never met.

This feeling of not being enough followed me into high school. When I met the boy whom I first gave my whole heart to, I thought, *Perhaps I am good enough!* I had two years of feeling better inside, valuable. But it appeared to be too good to be true. Right before my senior prom, he broke up with me. My world shattered into pieces and the walls I had let down — hell, almost forgotten — taunted me. I didn't understand why I wasn't good enough. In the early 90s there wasn't a lot of talk about mental health, but I am quite sure I entered into a depression which lasted almost two years.

"You stole my soul like a ghost in the movies.
I tried to fight it but, boy, you really moved me.
Six billion dollars couldn't rebuild this heart of mine.
Can't feel nothing now, except for this table wine."
— Train and Jewel: "Turn the Radio Up"

As I started college, I simply got lost in the crowd. I didn't make a lot of friends and spent a lot of time with "poor me" in my head. Then, my studies and future started to take shape. I was going to double major … no double DEGREE it! I would have a B.A. in Communications and a B.A. in German Language and Literature. I was certain this was right. My spirit embraced my dreams and propelled me forward with great momentum and I was happy. The

German degree also came with one year studying abroad at a university in Germany. This was exactly what I needed to re-focus my energy and thoughts. That is exactly what I did.

Fast forward 15 years, two divorces, a beautiful daughter, and an eight-year stay in Germany, that same boy who first broke my heart breezed back into my world. It was a perfect storm. I felt the walls I had been building, perfecting, and repairing over the years simply fizzle into a pile of dust. I thought it must be fate, it must be … something. And that it was, my friends. Long-distance relationship, a bumpy move to a new state, expectations unspoken, a wedding, a birth of another beautiful daughter, and the purchase of a new house twisting, turning, and spinning like leaves in the breeze, laced with ugly energy. It lasted two years officially and if you felt my despair as a high school senior, multiply it by 100. My entire being screamed. I thought for sure I wouldn't make it through the darkness that came for me.

But I did. The light did break through and was always there. My girls and I healed, slowly. I went through all of the stages of grief, until finally there was nothing left but me. There I was. I closed my eyes and remembered so many great and wonderful things about me. I heard the whispers of accomplishments and perseverance. I felt the joy and love overflow when I looked at my girls. I felt my mother's wisdom in my core. I saw the fierce and true love I have to offer. I realized deep within that I could never allow anyone's opinion or love to define me, except for my own. Slowly, ever so slowly, I began to heal. As I did, I left "poor me" out with the trash and put on my sexy big girl panties, and I promised myself to be only me every day, to listen to my heart (and gut), and to shine my light bright in all directions. The disruption I needed to "see" my light was turbulent for certain. However, through it, I realized that the boy, well he couldn't love me how I needed or deserved to be loved, and the lesson I learned is to never stop listening to all my internal signals. I learned, finally, that I am more than good enough.

When did I dim my light? Well, lovies, I am afraid there was no one moment — rather, a series of moments, events, and feelings through which my internal light dulled. There is so much more to the story, of course, and it is all still here, with me. I learned so much along the way and I have met some amazing people, who I am eternally grateful for. My message, in this beautiful compilation, is to be brave.

Be brave and let go of any expectations there may be out there of how you should shine your light. Be brave and know that all you are and all you ever were, is one. Be brave and step into you. We are all here waiting to embrace your light, however and whenever it shines.

As for me, the train is still truckin' along and I am excited to love, learn and grow.

Take good care and stay fabulous.

About Heather Iden

A forever student of self, Heather Iden dabbles in poetry and short stories in stolen moments between working full time as an international human resources specialist, dealing with college woes and growing pains of her oldest daughter, and witnessing the delight in her youngest daughter as she puts on her first ballet shoes. For 30 years, Heather has lived, learned, studied, cried, laughed, gone on fabulous adventures, and drowned in dark times. With university, living abroad, creating a career, and becoming a mom behind her, Heather's voice of reflection tinted ever so gently with humor has emerged. Stay tuned, for there is more to come!

Acknowledgments

I want to thank each of the women who decided to be vulnerable and expose their heart felt journeys to the rediscovery of their authentic selves. Releasing societal expectations, conditioning and heartaches is not an easy path. Shifting from "why is this happening to me?" to "how am I supposed to learn from this challenge?" is monumental growth for anyone. Each of the women in "Soul Shine" has taken a deep, dark look into their lives and their soul, to excavate the gifts and purpose that each was always meant to be for this world. Putting our struggles into words and sharing with each of you has also been a healing and cathartic process. I hope you have found comfort, inspiration, and a spark of fire to guide you on your soul rejuvenation. I also hope you find gratitude for each of the contributors of Soul Shine, for shining their light and illuminating a path for you!

About the Author

Along her healing journey, Carrie Myers realized that she made herself small and dulled her shine for the comfort of others. The reality is that most people do, especially women. In our efforts to "be good" and acceptable, we shrink ourselves. Carrie knew it is time to tell our stories, share our struggles and then break free of the shadows. Along with 25 other amazing, vulnerable, and powerful women, she exposes her heart and strives to create a consciousness around the tragedy of women not claiming and fully living in their soul's purpose.

It is time we all shine our brightest.

To learn more about Carrie and her soul's purpose visit carriemyersauthor.com and yourselfprogram.com

Ingram Content Group UK Ltd.
Milton Keynes UK
UKHW022236080323
418264UK00013B/761

9 781913 590710